Tricky Puzzles for Brainy Kids

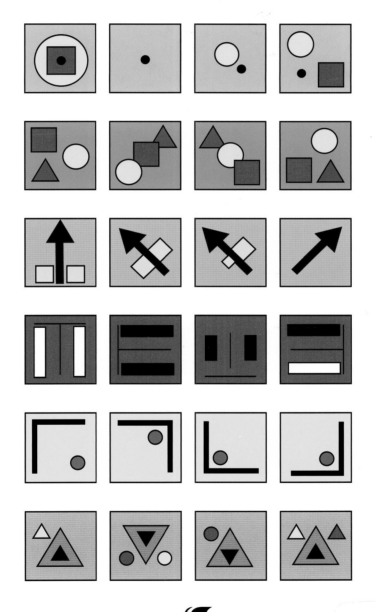

Sterling Publishing Co., Inc.
New York

3rd grade and summer 2005

Puzzles by Christiane Krapp
Illustrations by Bianca Peters

Published by Sterling Publishing Co., Inc.
387 Park Avenue South, New York, N.Y. 10016
Excerpted from the books *Gehirnjogging für Kinder Logiktraining I. Klasse;
Gehirnjogging für Kinder Logiktraining. 2 Klasse; Gehirnjogging für Kinder
4. Klasse* © 2001 Edition Bucherbar im Arena Verlag GmbH.
English translation © 2003 by Sterling Publishing Co., Inc.
Distributed in Canada by Sterling Publishing
C/o Canadian Manda Group, One Atlantic Avenue, Suite 105
Toronto, Ontario, Canada M6K 3E7
Distributed in Great Britain and Europe by Chris Lloyd at Orca Book
Services, Stanley House, Fleets Lane, Poole BH15 3AJ, England
Distributed in Australia by Capricorn Link (Australia) Pty Ltd.
P.O. Box 704, Windsor, NSW 2756, Australia

Sterling ISBN 1-4027-0549-2

Dear Parents:

School and everyday life demand a multitude of mental abilities from children. In sports it goes without saying that the body must be trained. But a targeted training is also imperative for the mind in order to meet all these mental demands. The puzzles in this book have been designed to build up the ability to think, independent of any educational pedagogy and classroom content.

Based on the newest developments in intelligence psychology and brain research, these exercises do not follow any specific learning strategy but rather develop the basic mental efficiency of the child. Through training the brain, learning is generally made easier. Many exercises lend themselves well to repetition and the incentive is, as with any other kind of training, a sense of achievement.

The exercises are fun and stimulate important brain functions:

- Visual perception
- Memory
- Quick understanding
- The ability to recognize connections
- The ability to draw the right conclusion

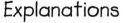

Explanations

The first tasks are kept simple to guarantee an effortless entry into the exercises.
The instructions are deliberately short and formulated concisely so that the child can work with the book even without outside help. Answers are in the back, so the child can feel the satisfaction of verifying his or her success.

As you would with physical training, you can also keep track of the child's progress with these techniques. After some practice, the child's success becomes visible here as well. In one exercise, the child grasps the principles required to perform the first task. Compare the time it takes for the first task with the time needed for the challenges that follow! And the child will become comfortable using many of these techniques in the standardized tests that he or she will take later on.

In most cases, a soft pencil is all you need to solve the tasks. For others, colored pencils or crayons are required. These exercises may be repeated as often as you like. Every time they are performed, the puzzles will be solved faster and more easily.

Christiane Krapp

Getting Trees Together

Pair up the trees on this page with their mirror images. Give the two parts that belong together the same number. Write your answers in the empty boxes on page 5.

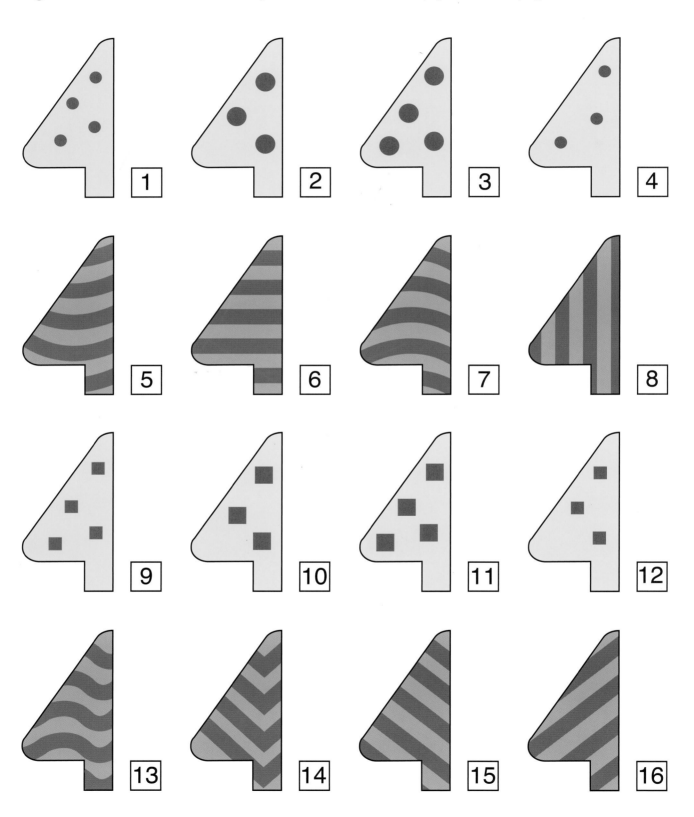

SarahAnne

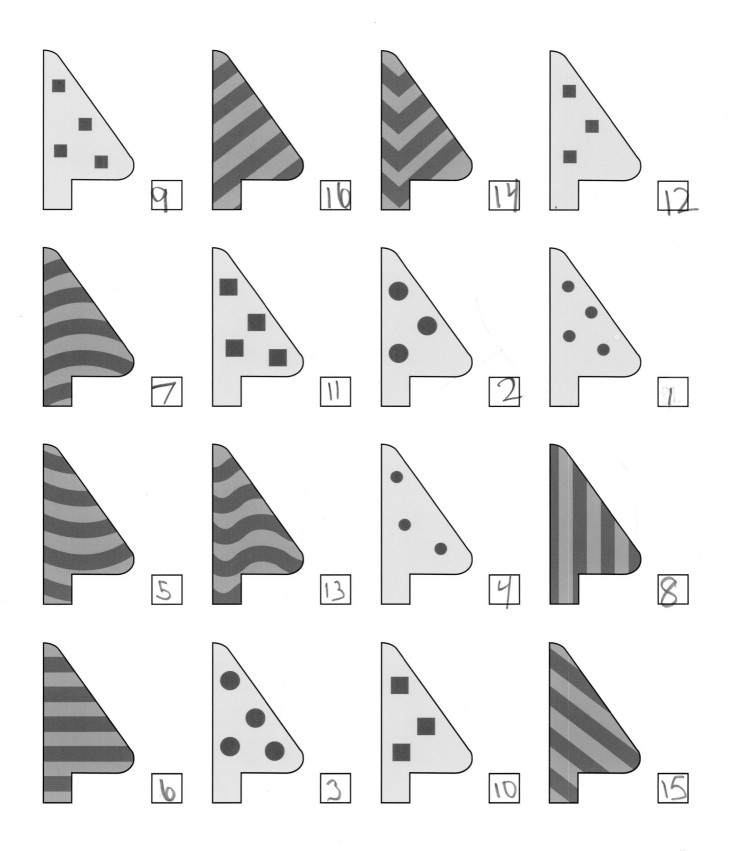

5

Ornaments

Which ornament do you get when you put together the individual parts?

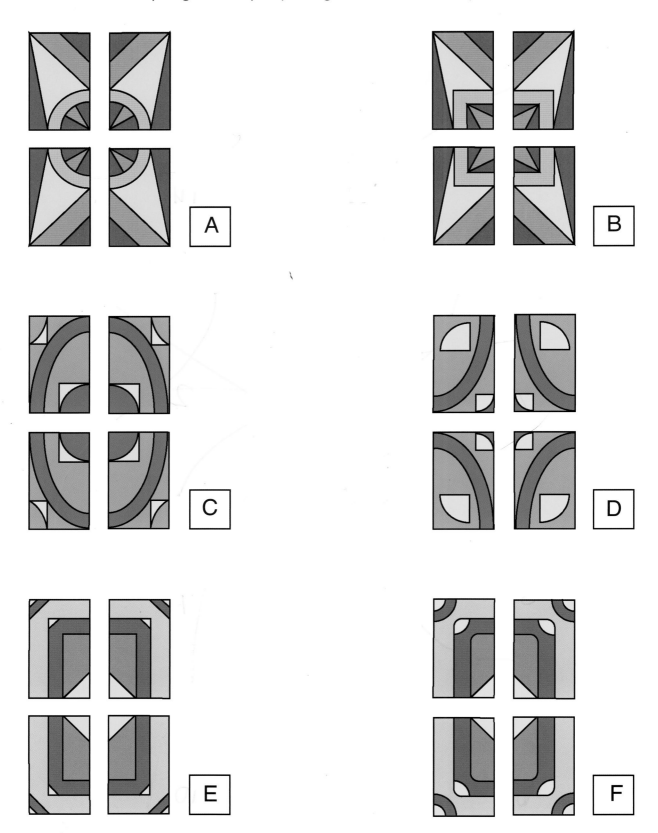

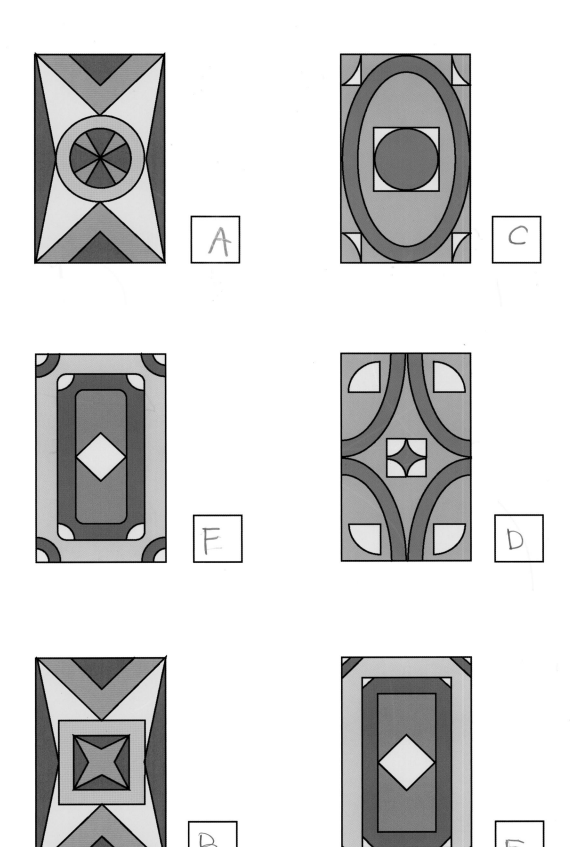

A

C

F

D

B

E

Lost Fishes

Mother and child have lost sight of each other.
Bring them together once more by connecting them with a line!

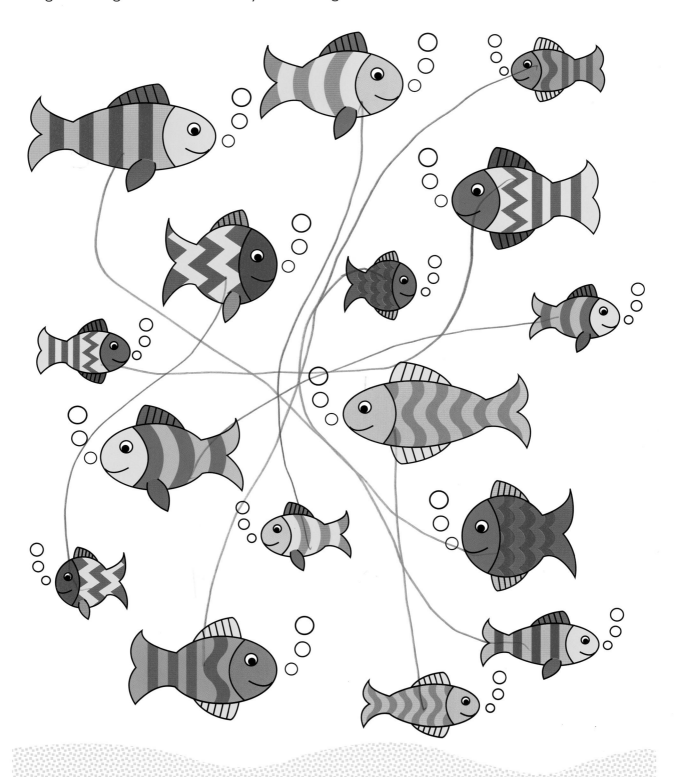

Sarah Anne

Lost Seahorses

Father and child have lost sight of each other.
Bring them together once more by connecting them with a line!

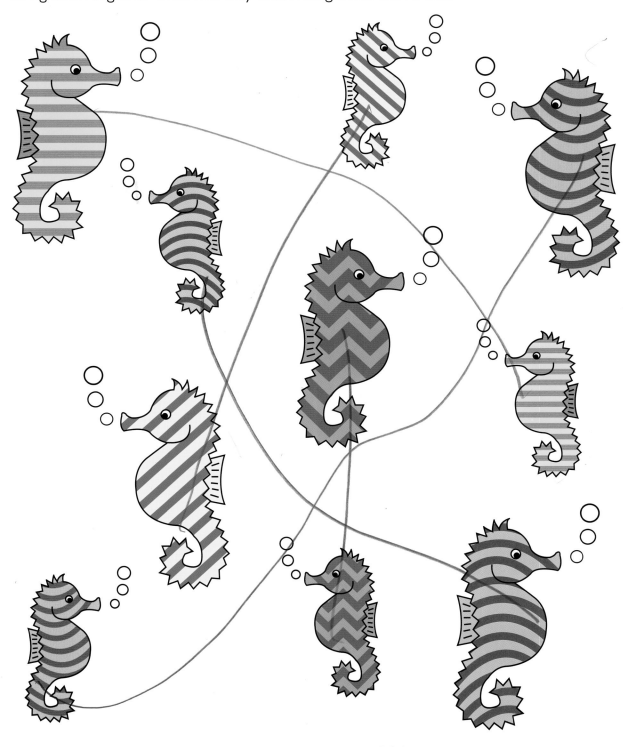

Trailer Trucks

Find the right trailer for each truck and write down your answers on the signs on page 11.

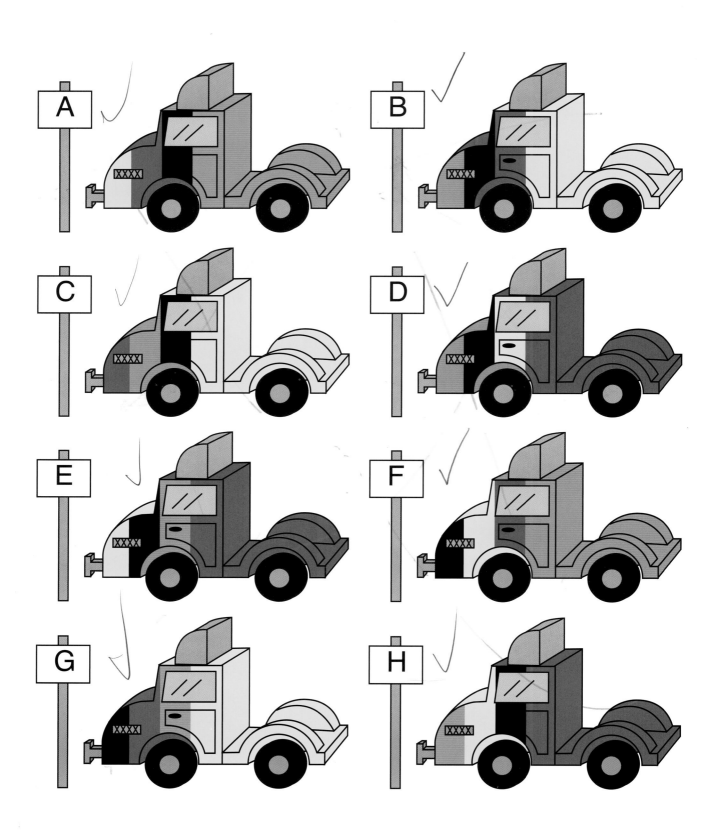

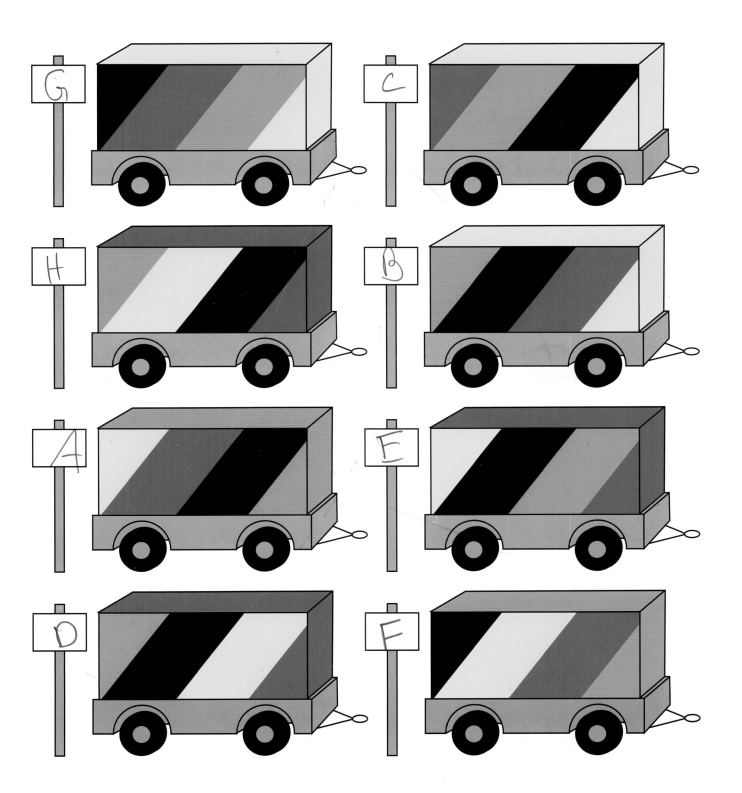

Sarah Anne

Penguin Twins

Match up the penguins on this page with their twins on page 13. Write your answers in the circles beneath the twins.

SarahAnne

What Is Johnny Going To Do Next?

Take your time looking at each picture! What is Johnny doing? What will he do next? Find out by searching the next page for the companion picture! Write your answer in the empty box.

Find the Right Roof

Select the right roof for each house. Draw it in to make sure, and put its number in the little house box.

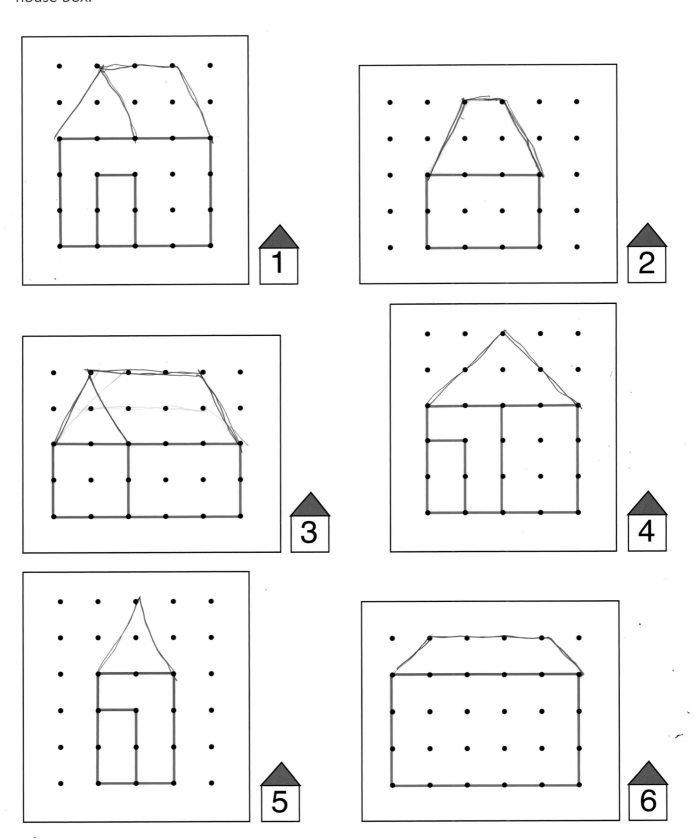

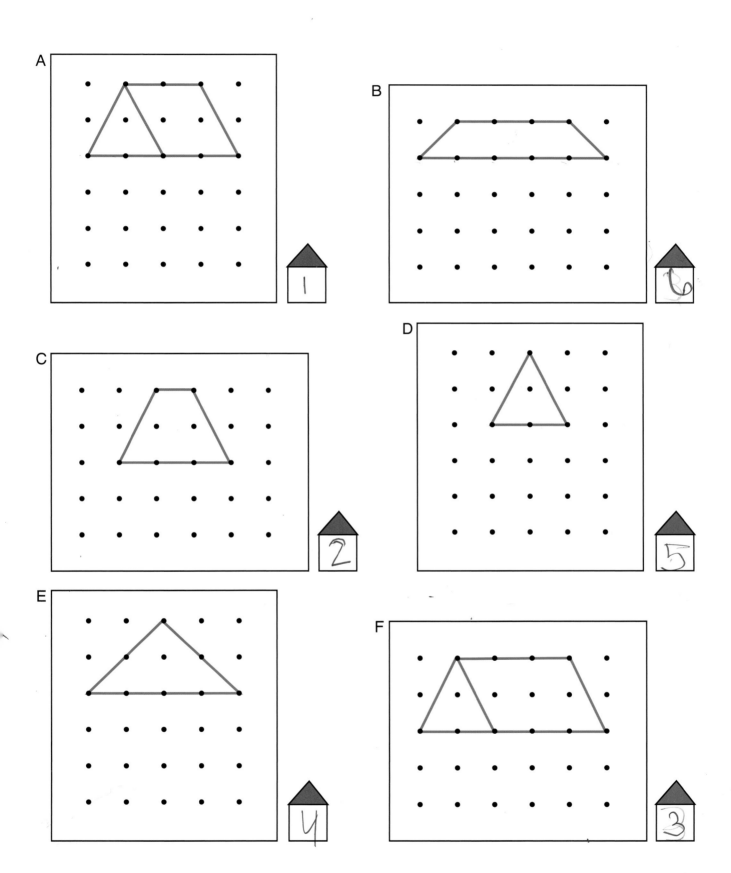

SarahAnne

Find the Missing Sock

Find the missing partner for each sock!

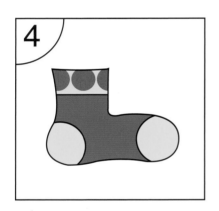

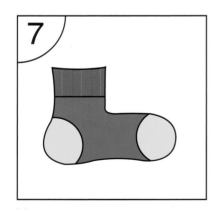

18

A 3

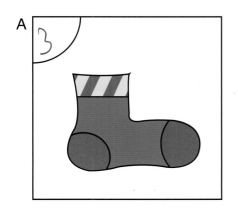

B 5

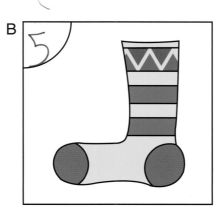

C 7

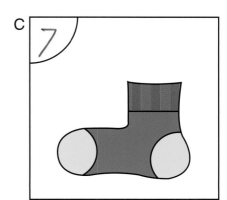

D 6

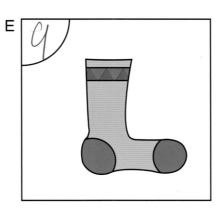

E 9

F 1

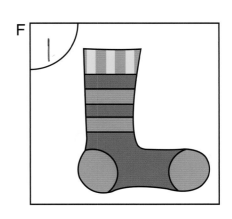

G 8

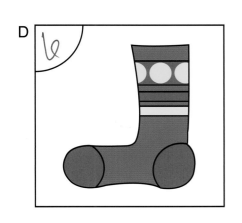

H 2

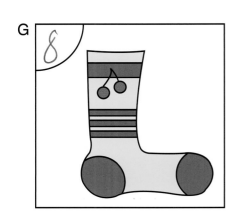

I 4

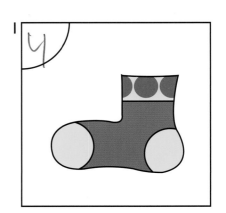

Sarah Anne

Complete the Picture Squares

Which shapes belong in the blank picture squares?
Write the letter and number in the circle below the missing signs on page 21.

1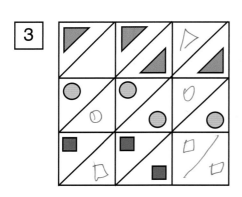

2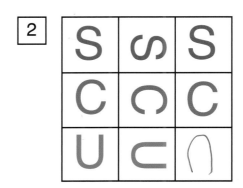

3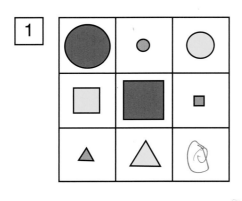

4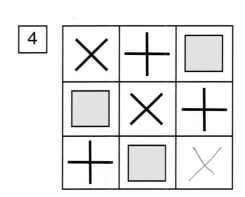

5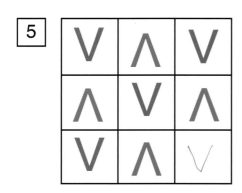

6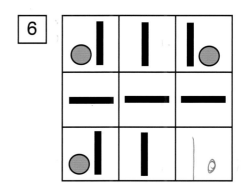

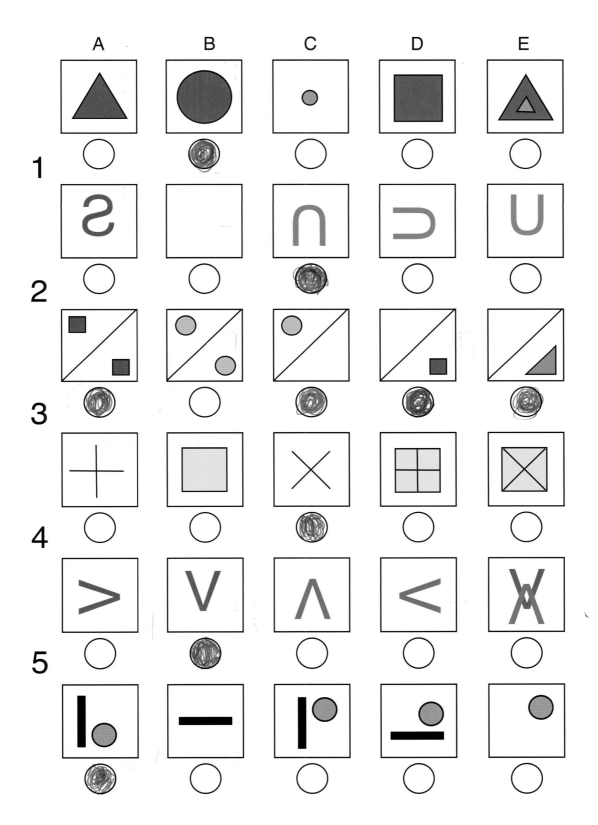

Complete the Rows

Three numbers are missing from each row. Can you figure out what those numbers should be?

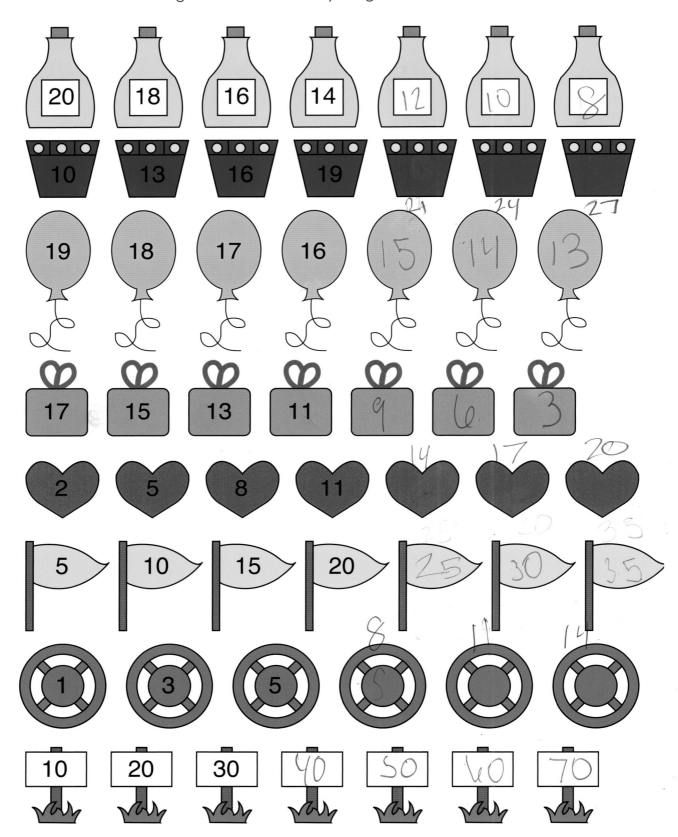

20 18 16 14 12 10 8

10 13 16 19

19 18 17 16 15 14 13
(21) (24) (27)

17 15 13 11 9 6 3

2 5 8 11 (14) (17) (20)

5 10 15 20 25 30 35
(25) (30) (35)

1 3 5 (8) (11) (14)

10 20 30 40 50 60 70

Cars

Which car does not belong in the row? Put an X in the circle beneath the car.

Road Plan

In each road plan, one piece is missing. Check the missing one in the circle below the plan.

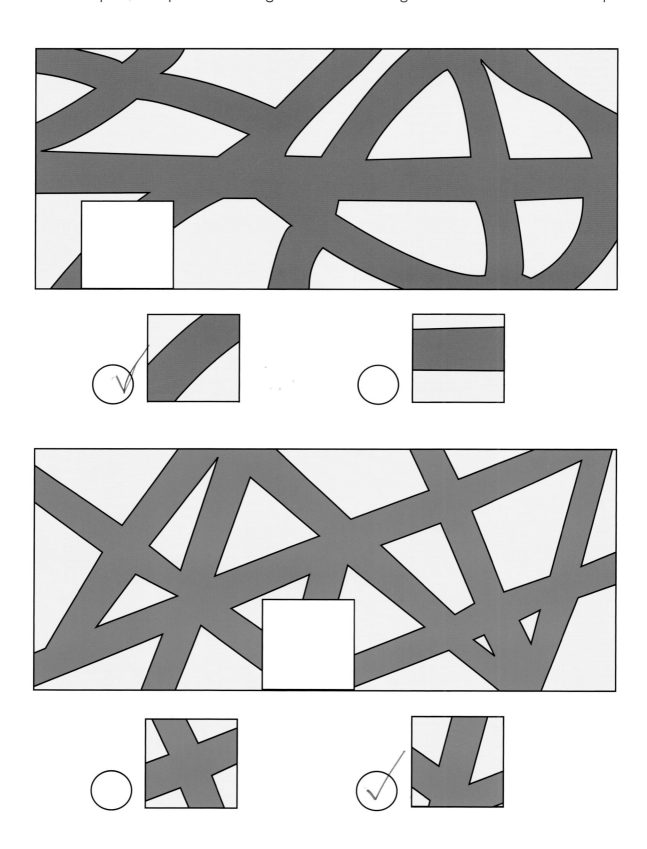

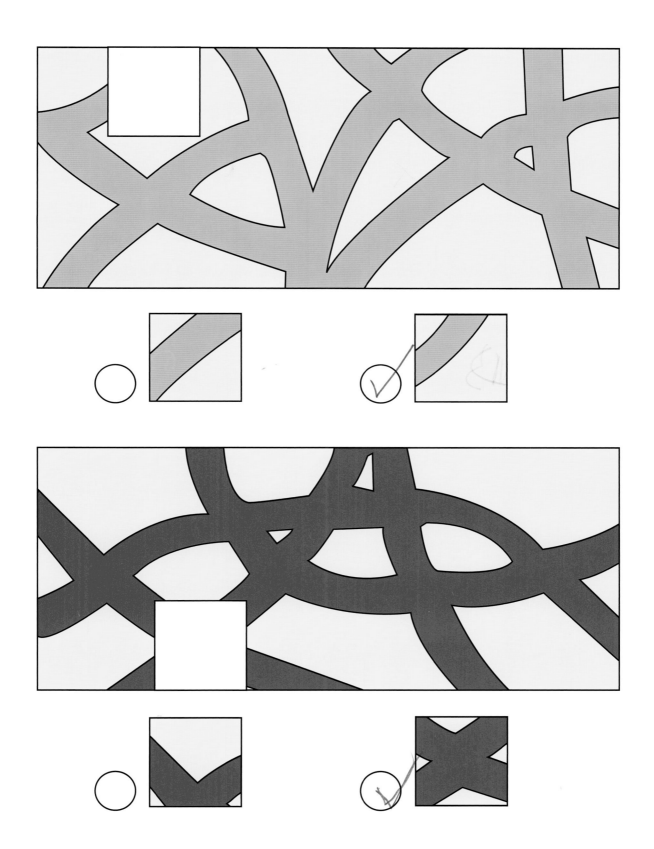

Trains

The sections of trains below belong to the trains on page 27. Figure out which train each section belongs with—A, B, C, or D.

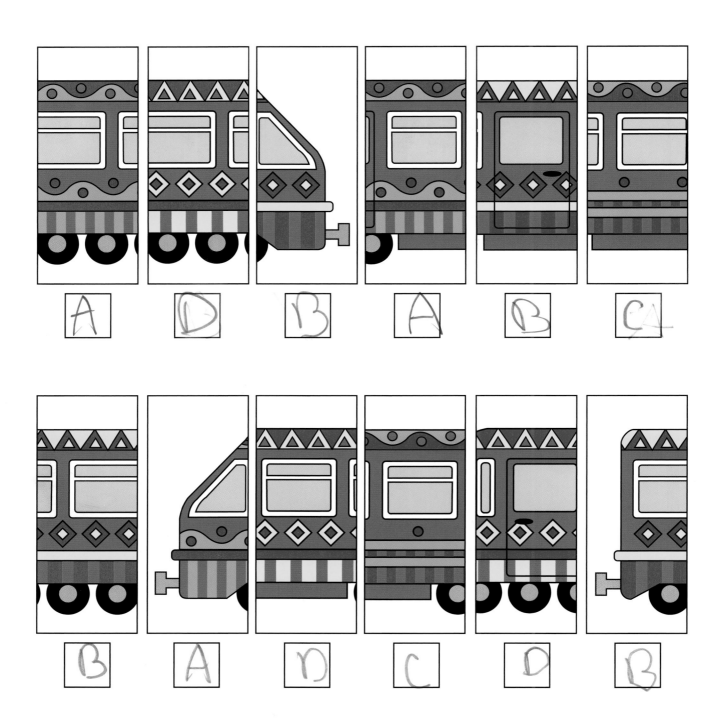

Row 1: A D B A B C

Row 2: B A D C D B

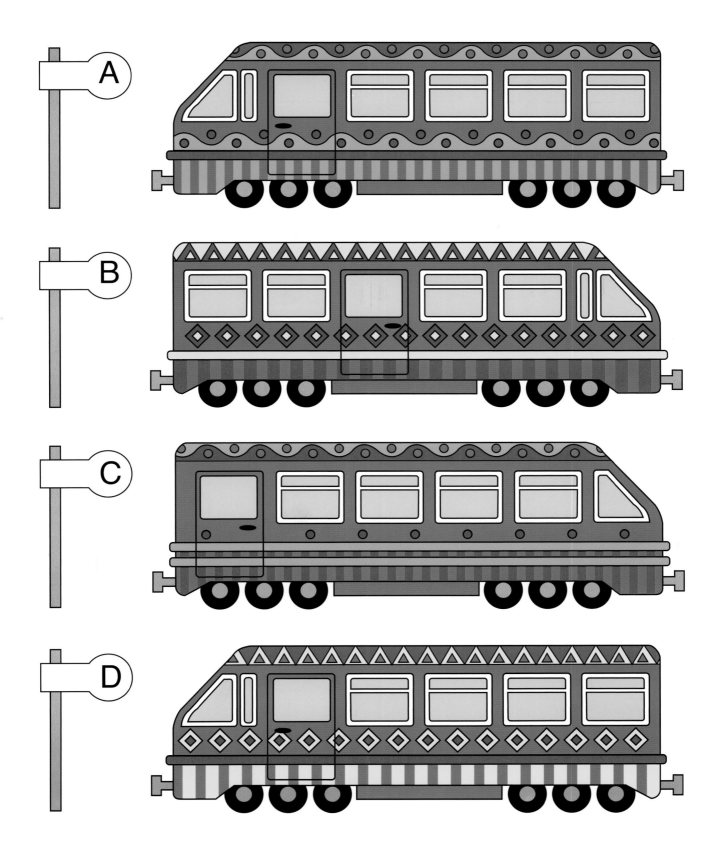

Pot and Lid

Which lid belongs to which pot? Write the letter of the pot on the little pot on top of the lid on page 29.

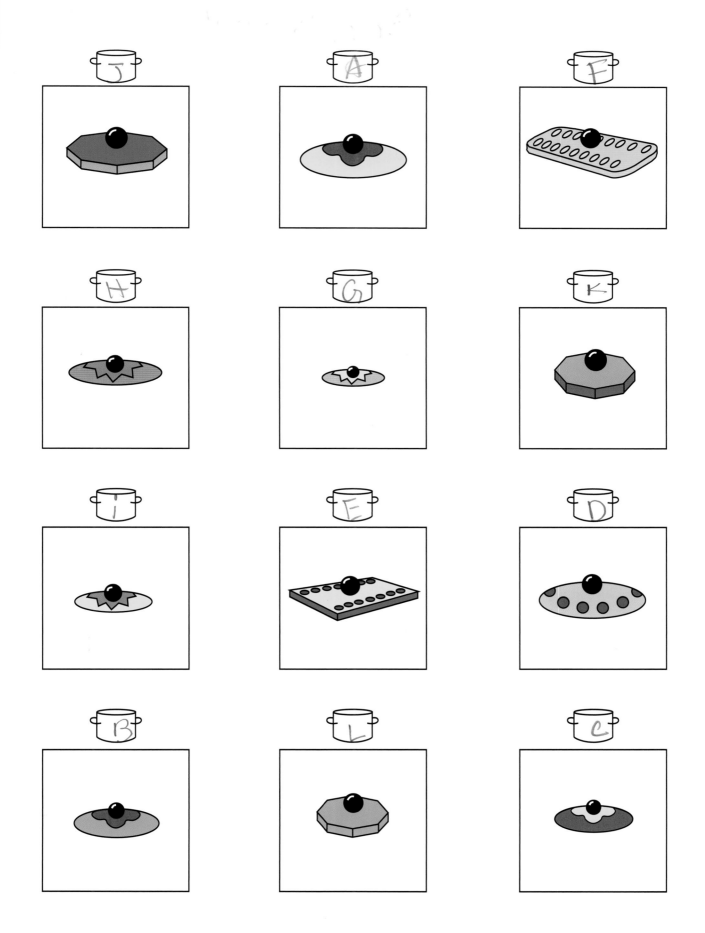

Which Is Tallest?

Put the pictures in each row in order by size. Start with the smallest illustration as #1.

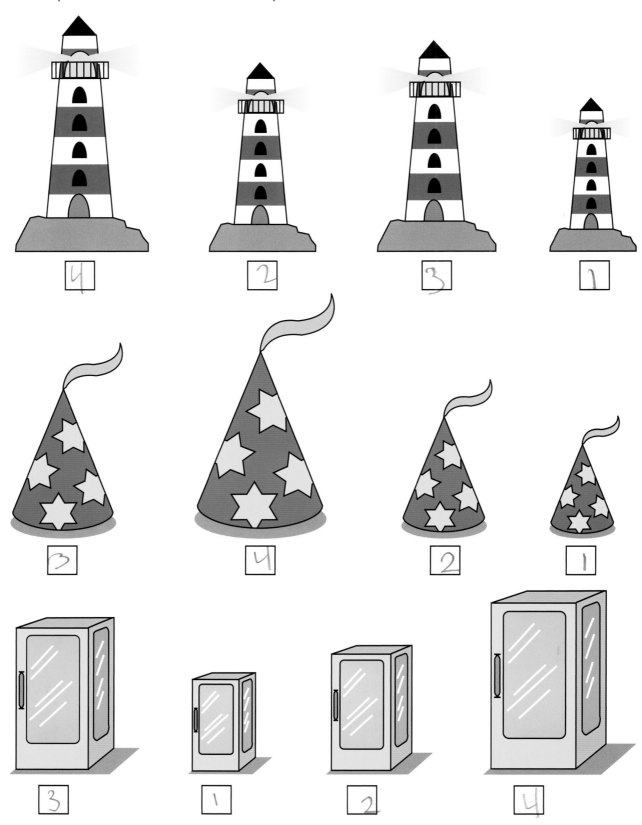

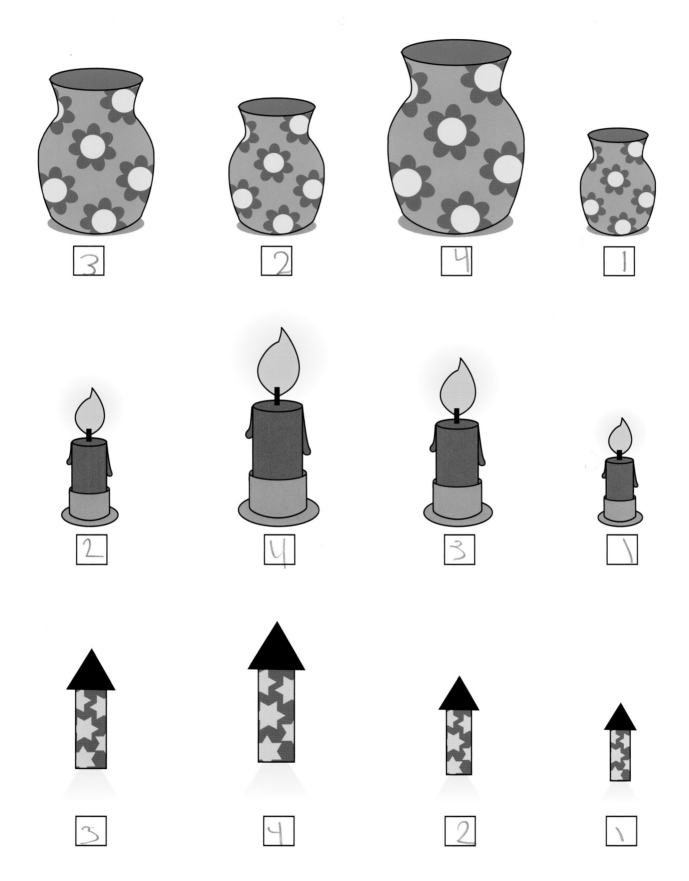

Who Is That?

Each set of boxes on page 33 is a jigsaw puzzle of one of these kids.
Can you unscramble them?

Paul

Liz

Josh

Ken

Adam

Hal

Jane

Ellen

Dan

32

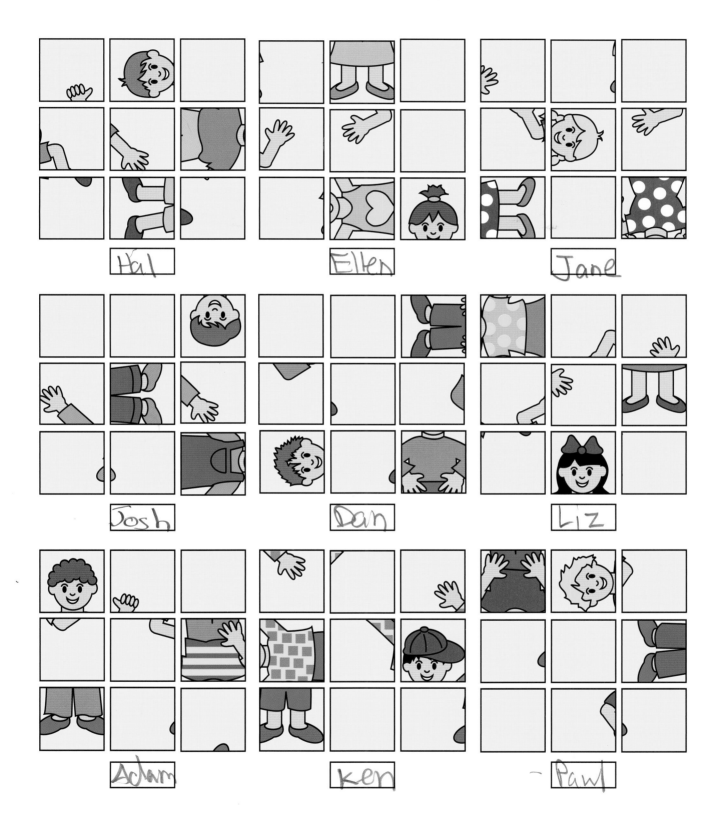

Hal

Ellen

Jane

Josh

Dan

Liz

Adam

Ken

Paul

33

Letter Squares

What letter fits in the empty space?

1

A	B	C
B	C	A
C	A	B

A	B	C

2

Y	O	X
O	X	O
X	O	Y

O	Y	X

3

P	b	B
B	b	P
P	b	B

b	P	B

4

C	O	C
Q	C	Q
O	Q	C

C	O	Q

5

L	E	F
L	F	E
F	L	E

L	E	F

6

X	Y	Z
U	V	W
R	S	T

W	T	X

34

Follow the Pattern

Which signs belong in the empty boxes? Put them in. Use colored pencils or crayons, if you have them.

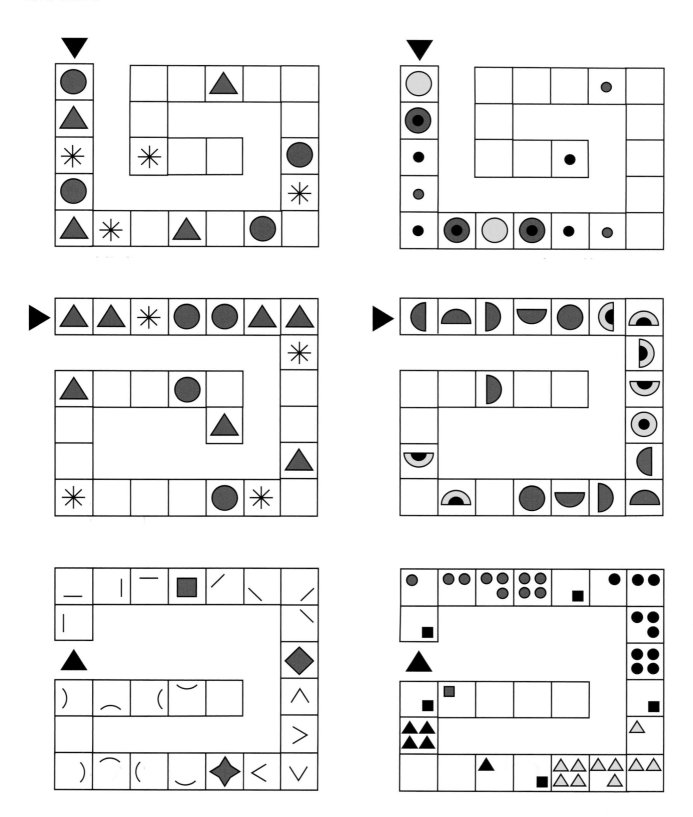

What Is It?

The vehicles on this page have been broken up into pieces on page 37. Can you recognize the vehicle from its parts?

1

2

3

4

5

6

A 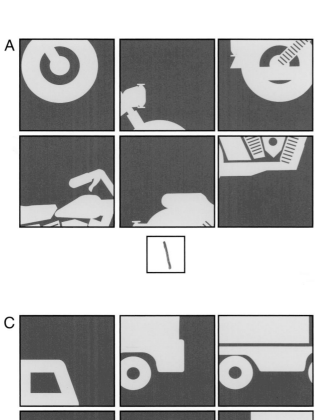 1

B 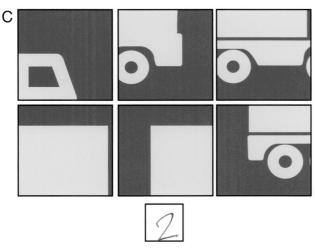 5

C 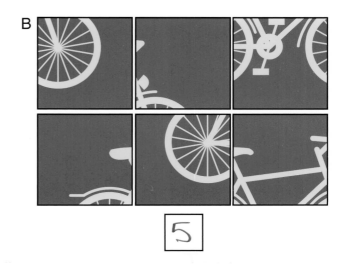 2

D 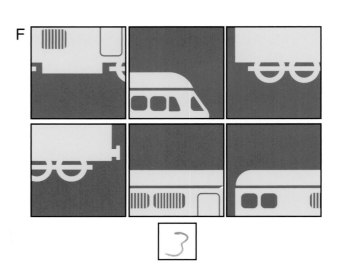 6

E 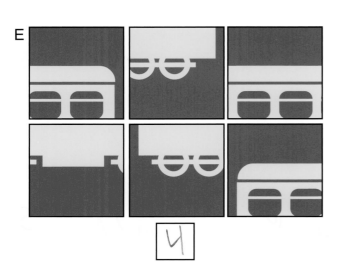 4

F  3

Picture Lotto

Where are the missing parts of these picture squares? Find them on page 39.

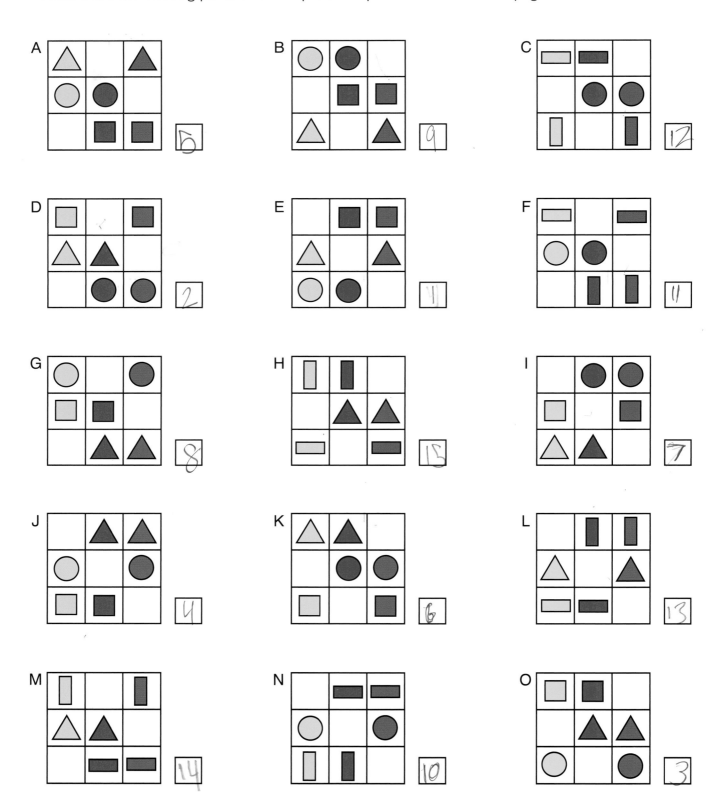

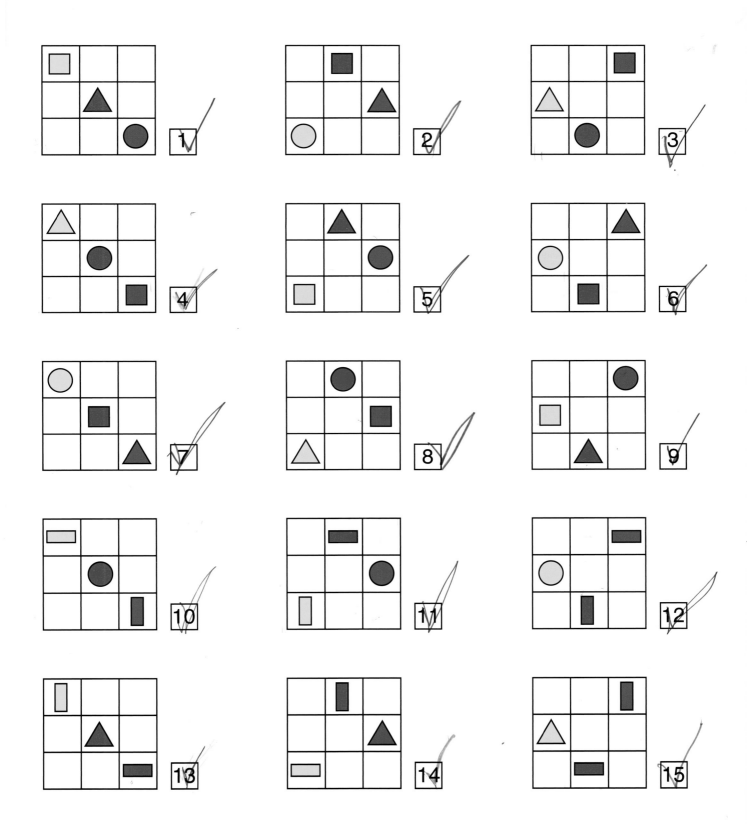

Find the Shape

Do you know which shape belongs in the empty box?
Choose it from among the shapes on page 41 and write down your answer in the small box.

SarahAnne

1 B

1 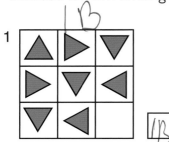 1B

2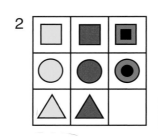

D 3

3 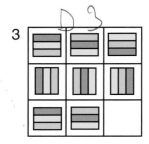 D3

4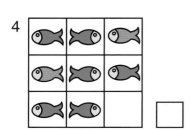

5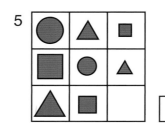

D 6

6 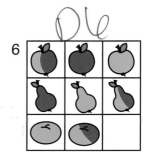 D6

7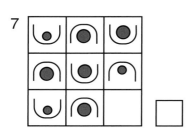

8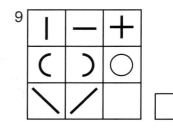

9

10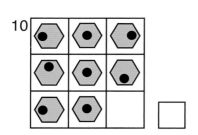

B 11

11 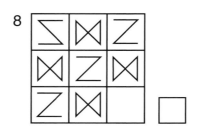 B11

12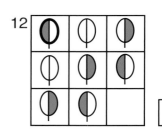

13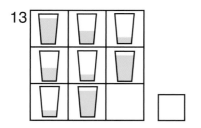

14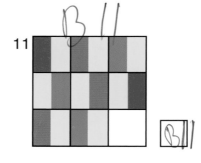

15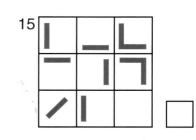

40

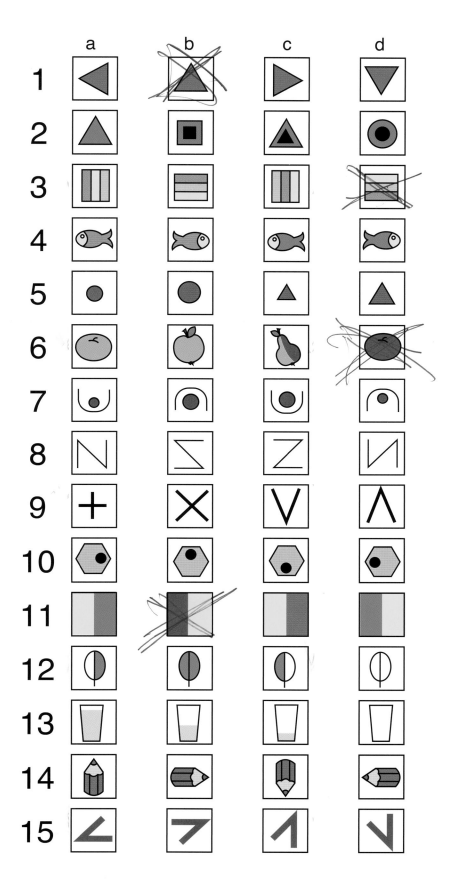

Completing Pictures

In each of these pictures, a colored area is missing. Look at the next page to see if the piece is pictured there. If it is, write its number in the small circle on this page.

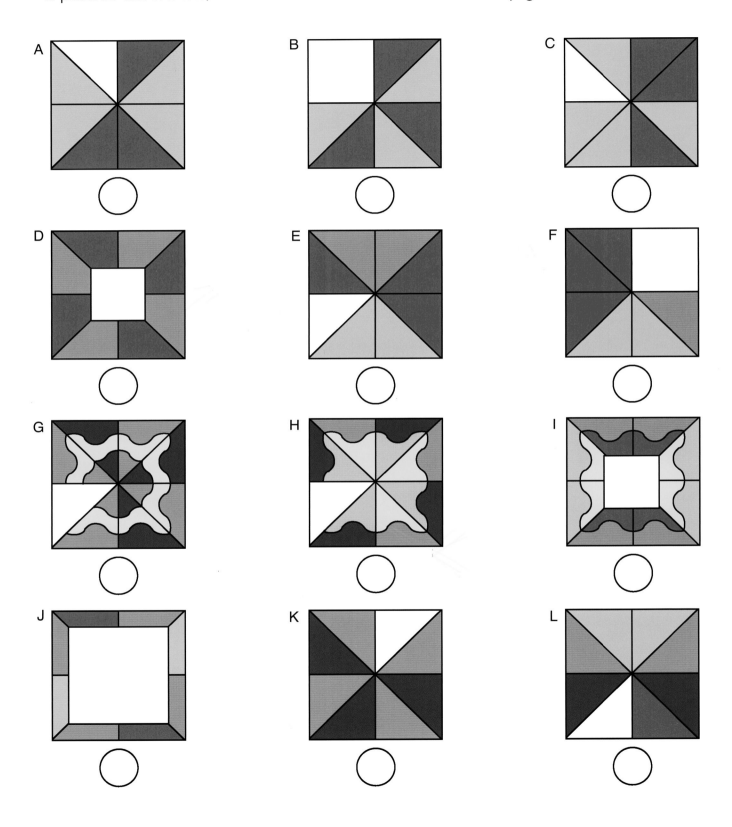

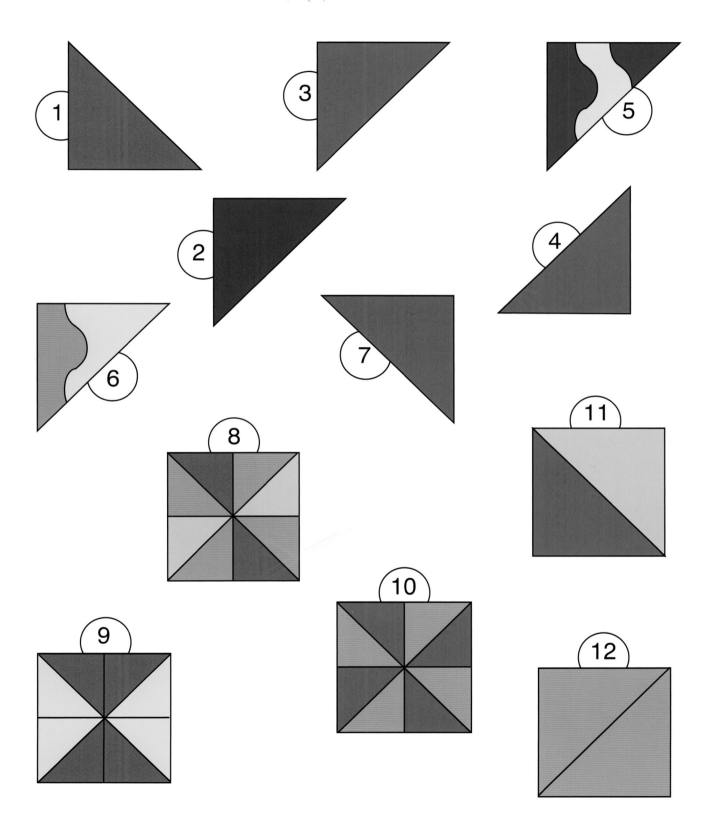

Mirror Images

If the line running down the center of the picture were a mirror, what would you see on the other side? Pair up the mirror images that go together.

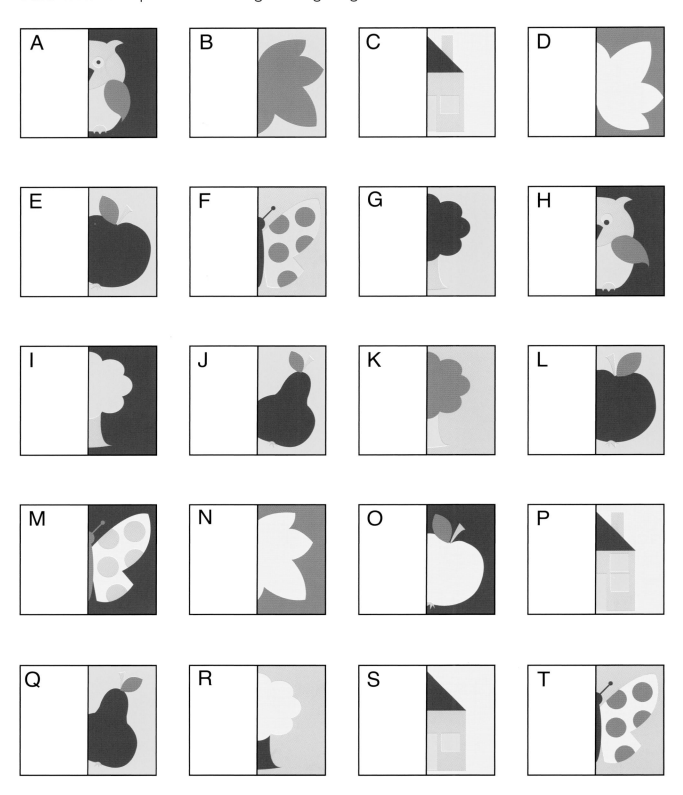

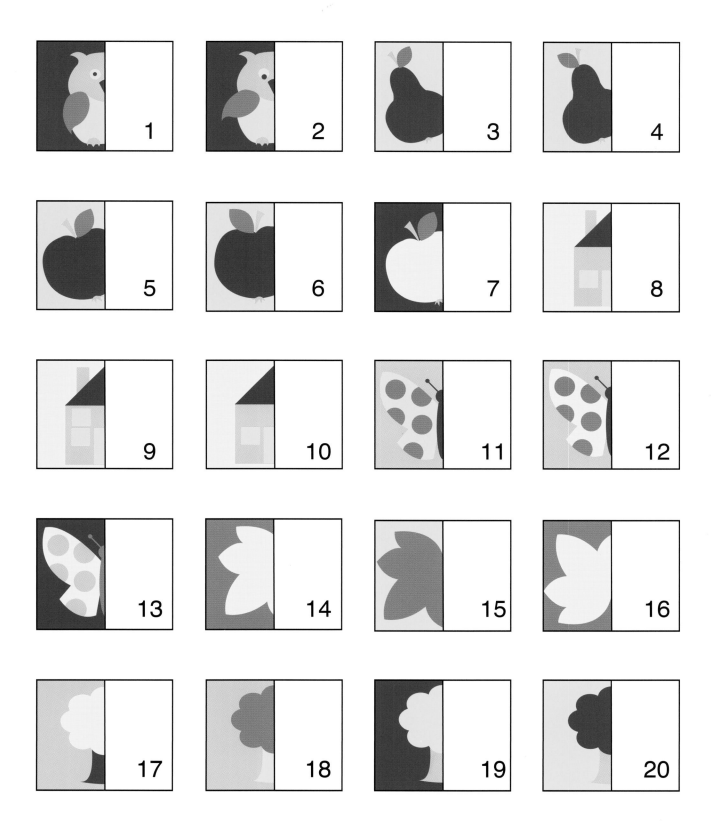

Easter Eggs

All the pictures on this page also appear on the next page, but in a different order. Can you match up the pictures that contain the same parts?

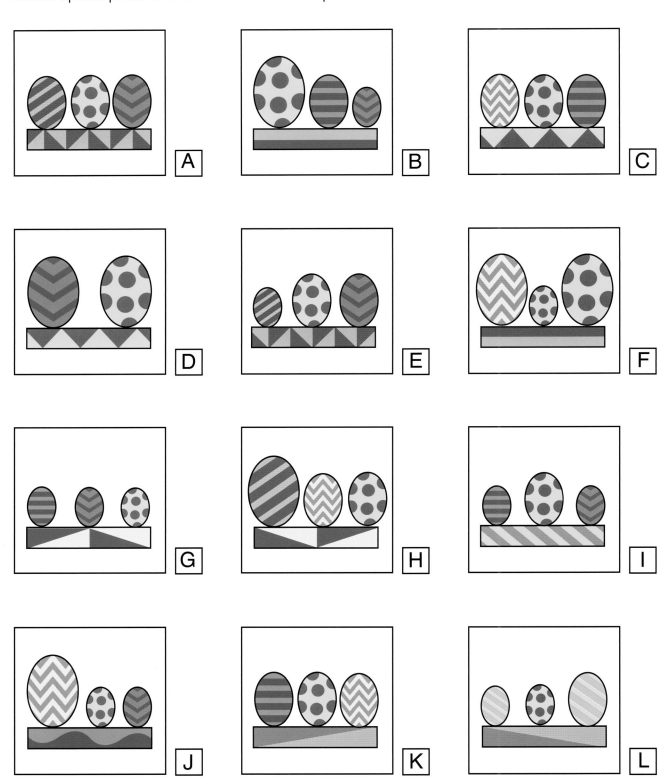

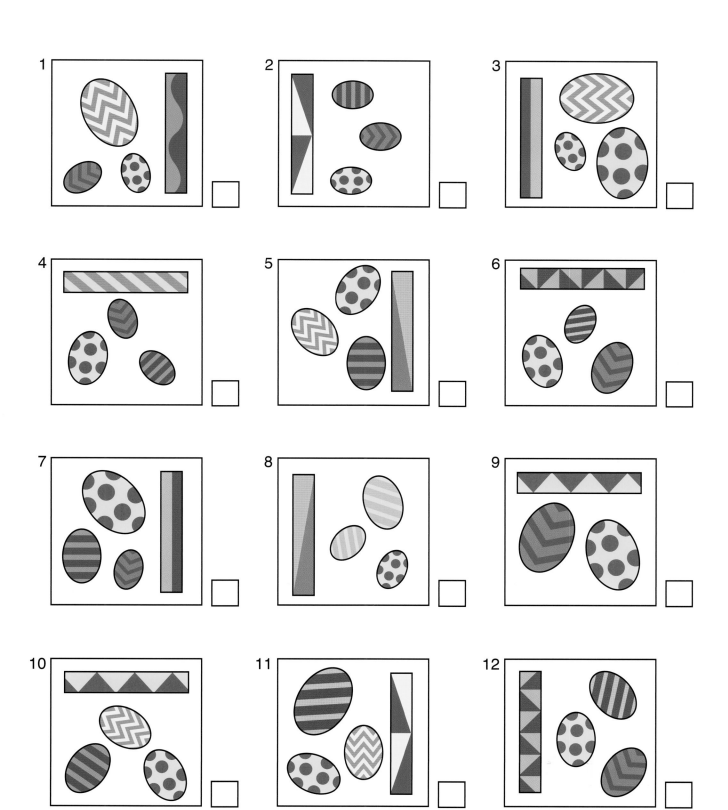

Picture Series

Select the picture that comes next for each one of the 5 rows.

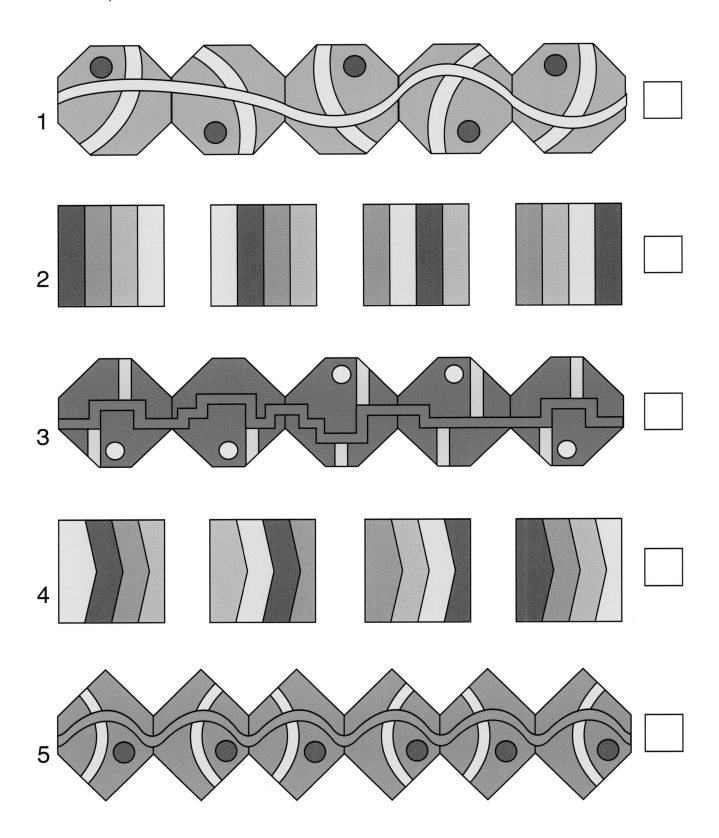

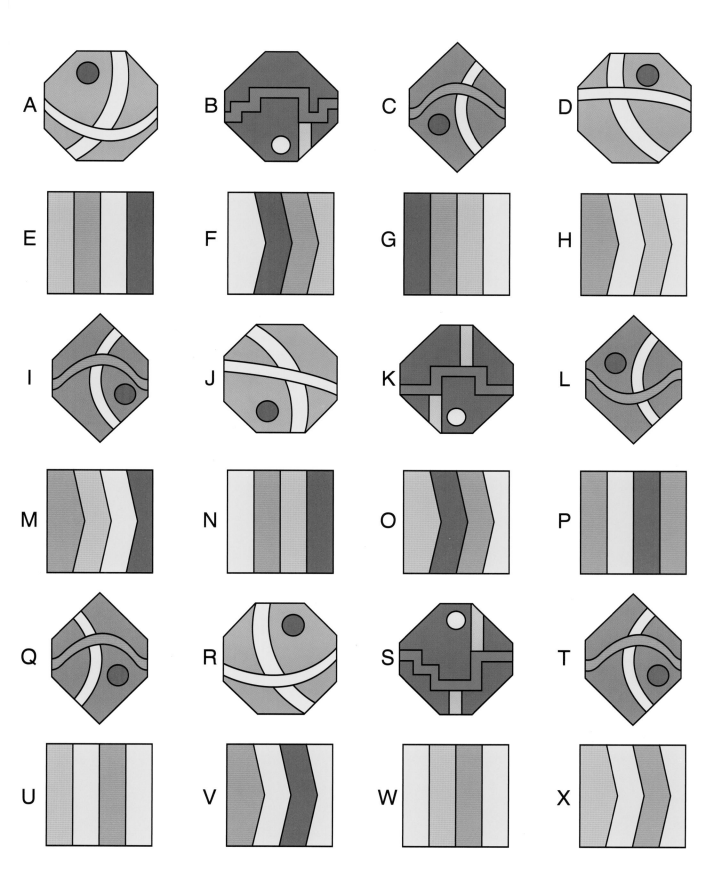

Crazy Parts

Each one of the 6 pictures is missing a part — but the parts are stretched out in a crazy way. Can you find the parts that come closest to fitting into the blank area?

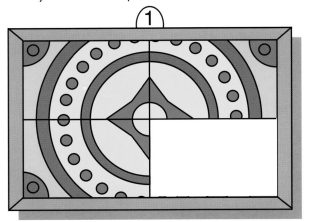

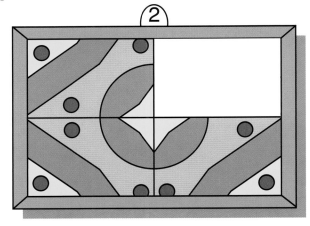

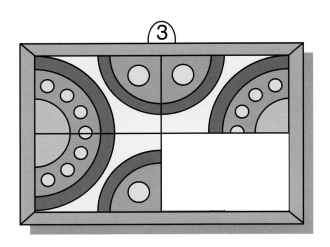

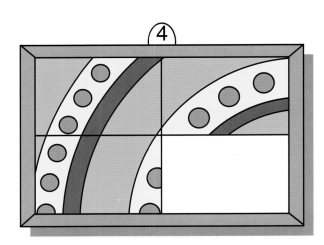

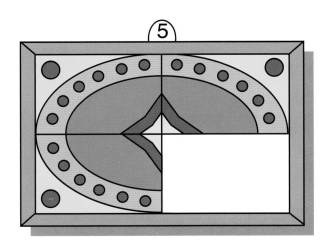

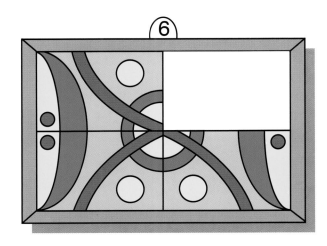

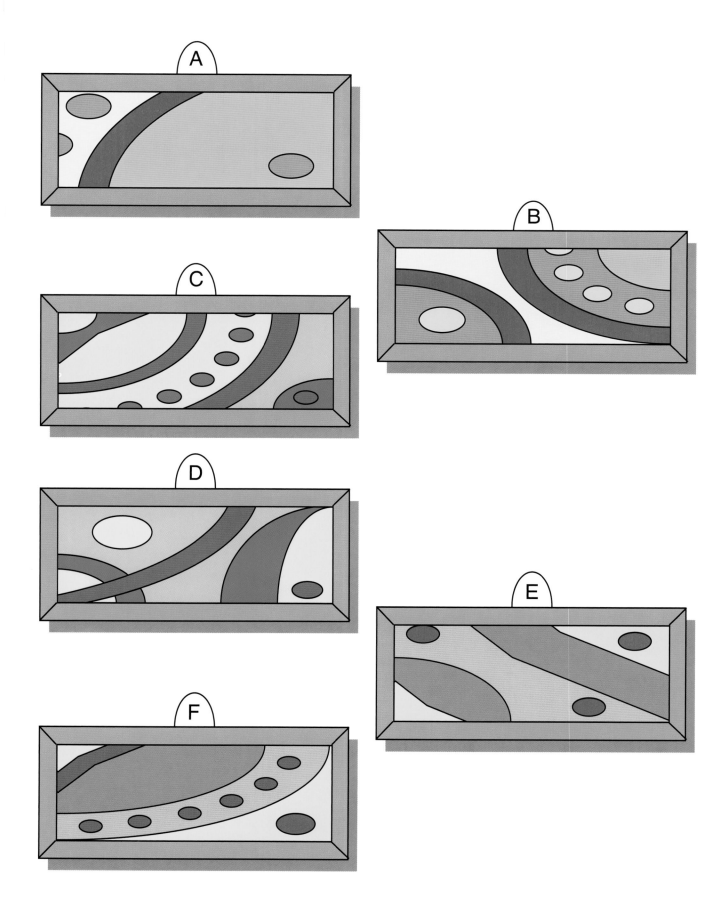

Sequences

Look carefully at the rows on these pages. They follow a certain order. Can you see what it is and how it changes? With colored pencils or crayons, draw in the next four pictures in each row that belong to each row.

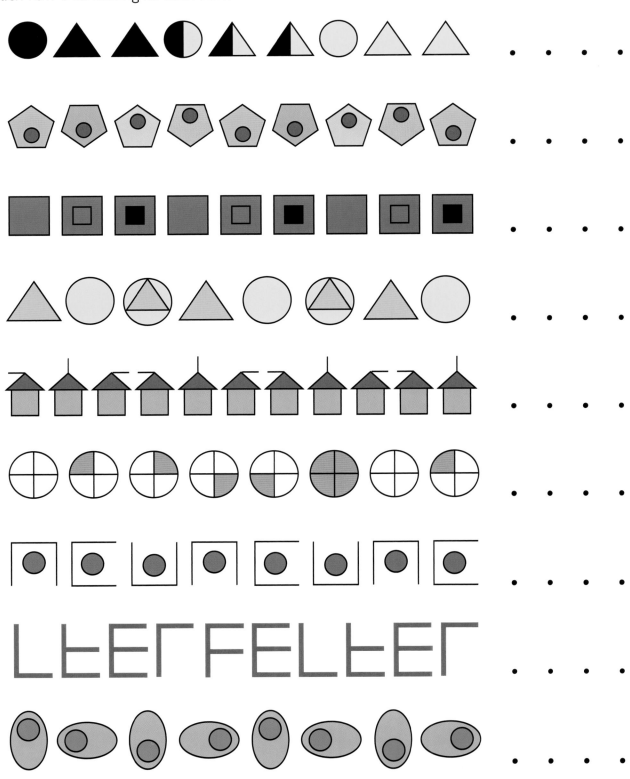

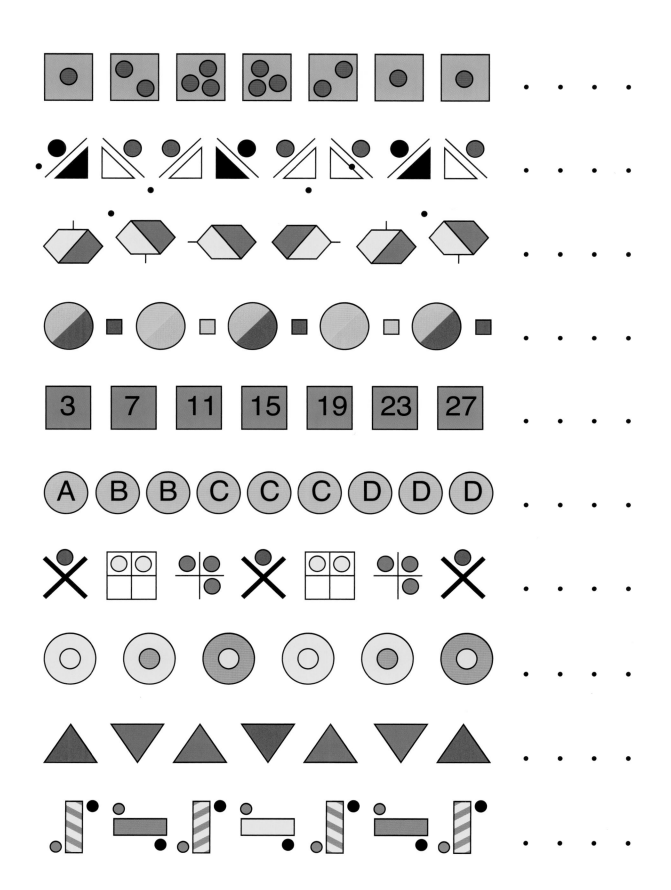

What Part Is Missing?

Find the right part to complete the picture. Place its number in the empty circles on page 55.

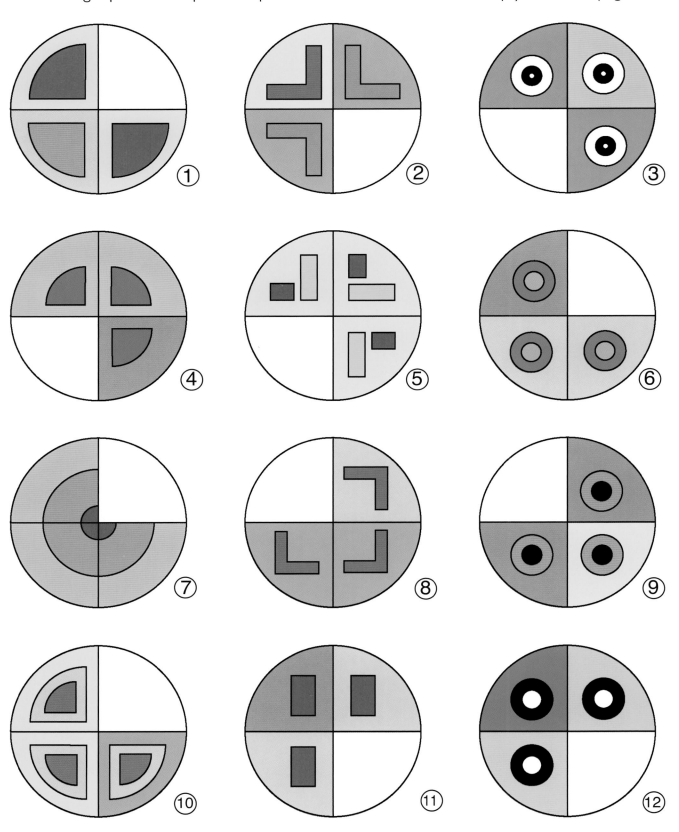

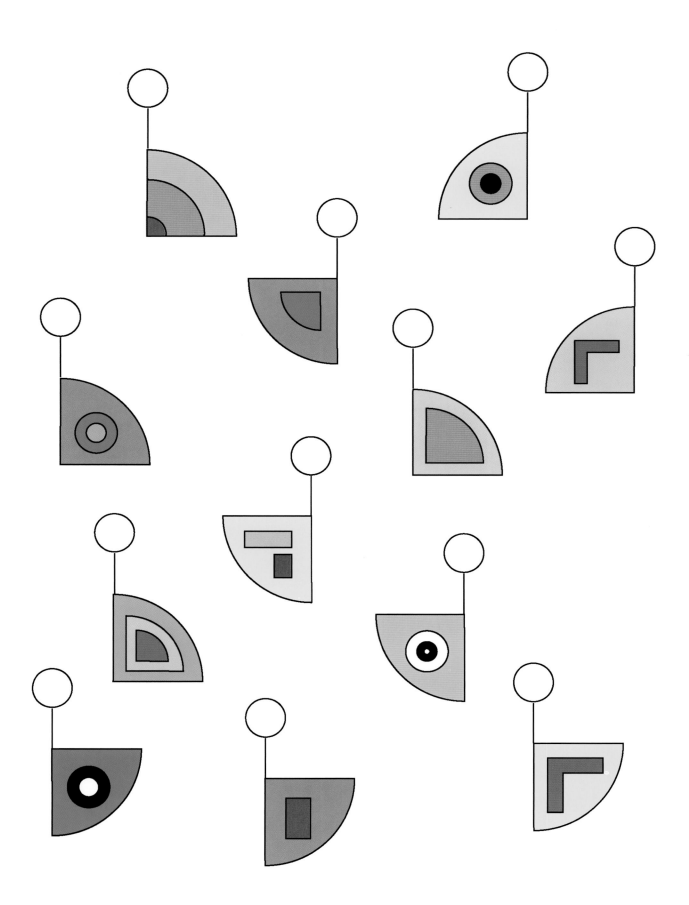

9-Part Puzzle

Where do the small cuttings from the picture belong? Write your answer in the little box beside the cutting.

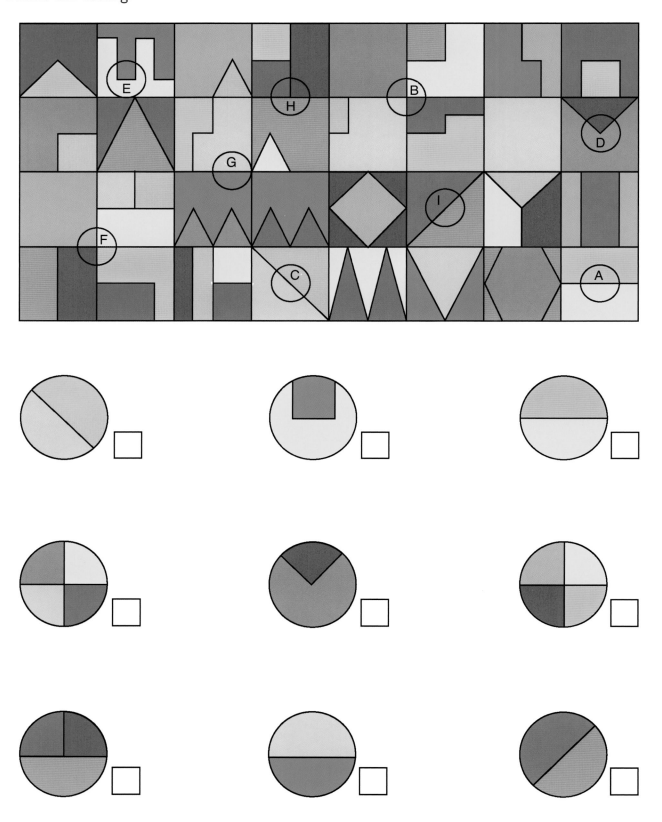

Color Squares

Which square is missing—A, B, or C?

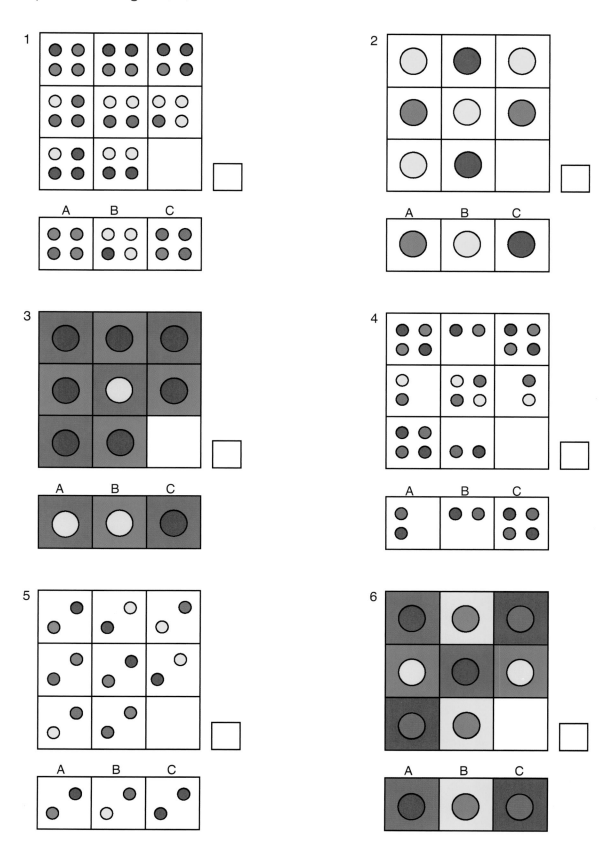

Putting It All Together

The individual little cards on this page result in 4 complete pictures if you put them together. But which picture do they belong to? Figure that out and write down the number underneath.

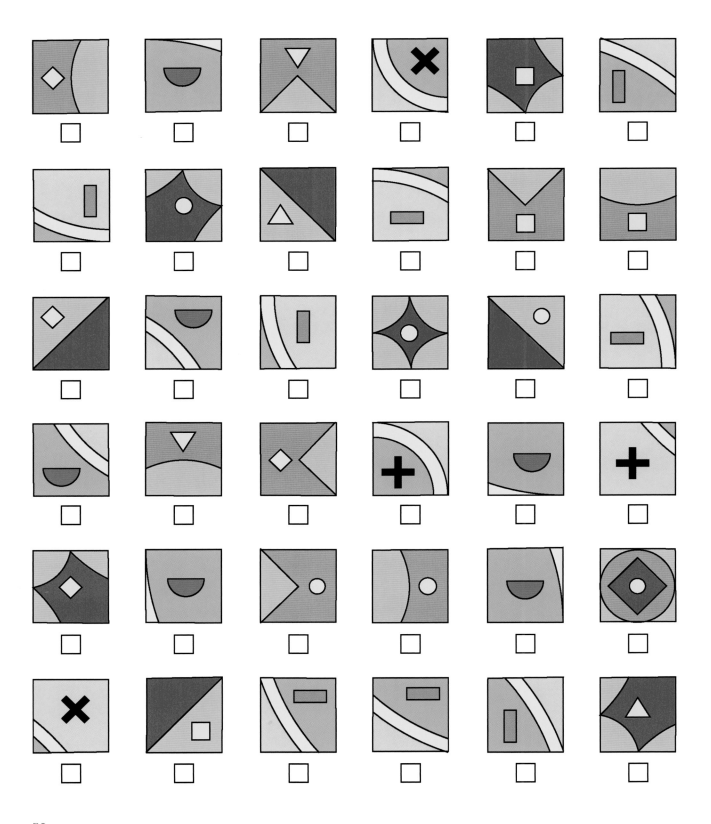

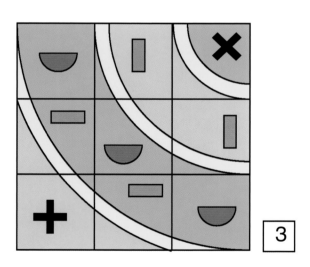

1

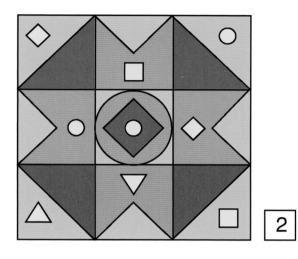

2

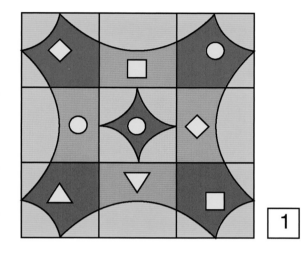

3

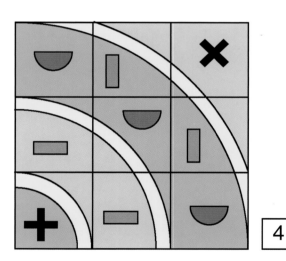

4

Flipped Hearts

Every picture on this page appears on the next page, but it has been flip-flopped. Where is it? Write the number in the empty heart.

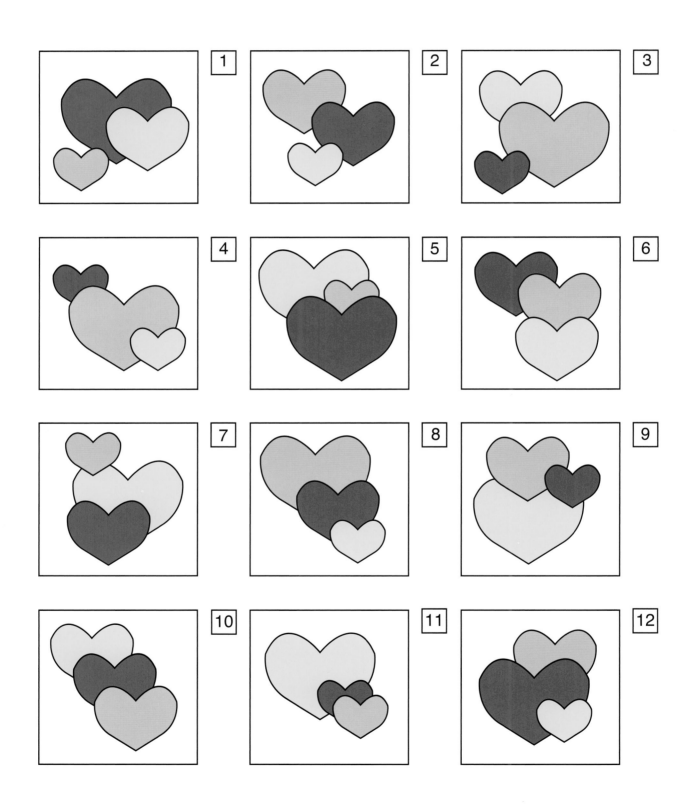

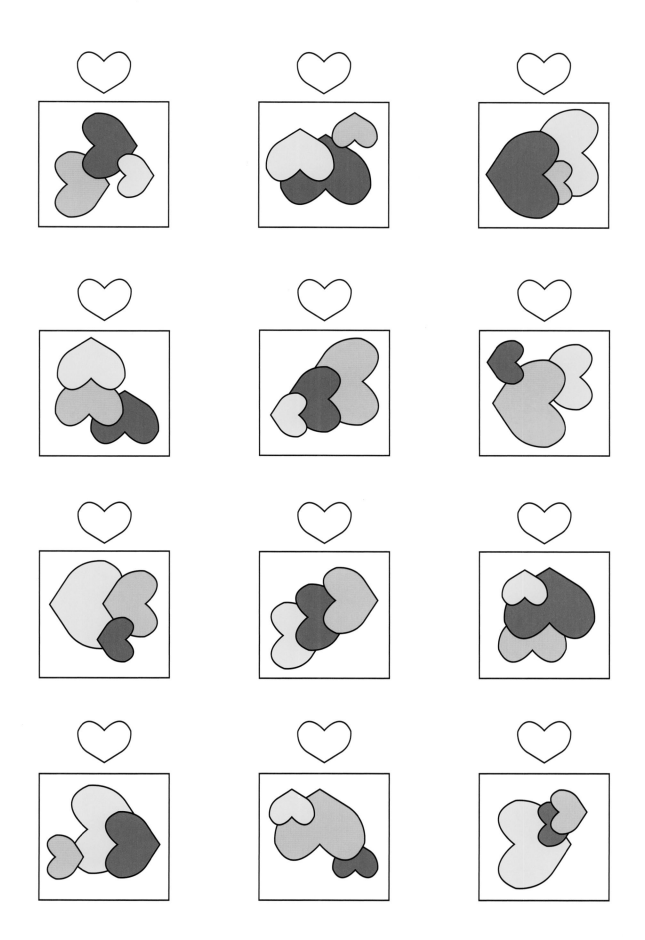

House Numbers

Three or four numbers are missing from each row of houses. Can you figure out what the numbers should be?

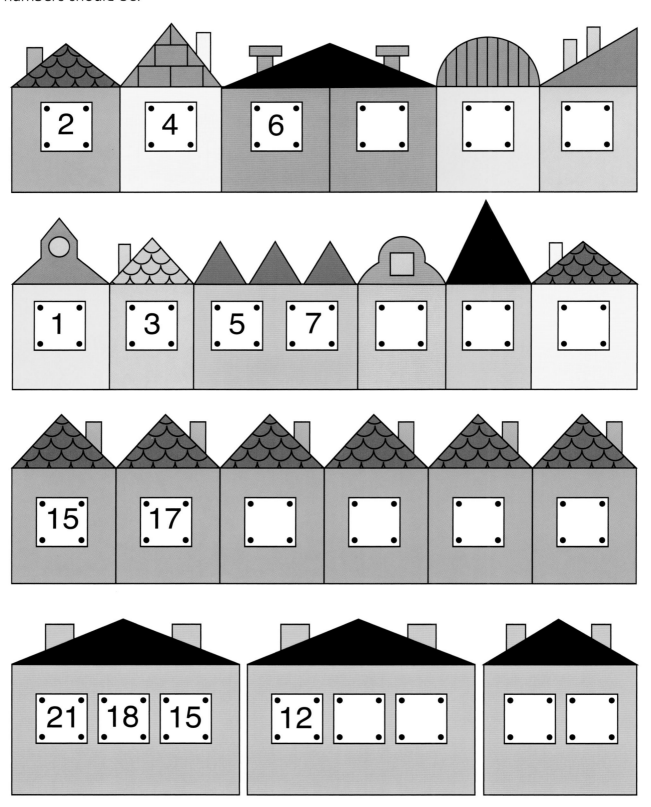

What's Wrong?

All the pictures in each row belong together — except for one in every row, which does not fit. Find it and circle it.

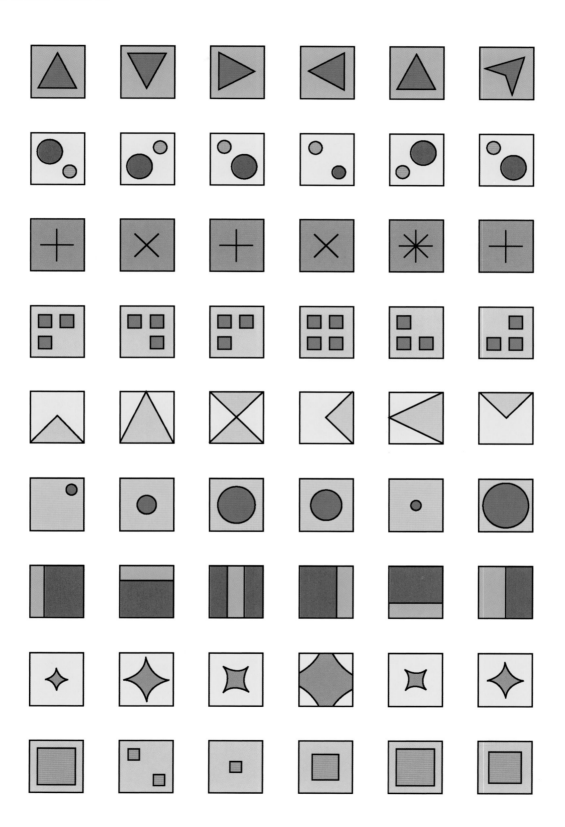

Windows

Most of the windows on this page are repeated on the next page, but with a difference. They have been stretched in one direction and shrunk in another—like this:

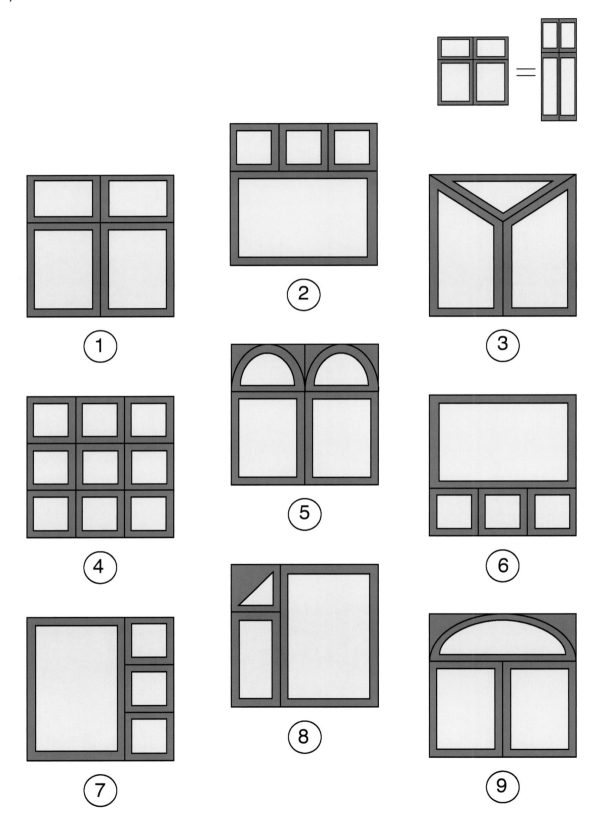

Which windows have the same pattern? If any don't match up, give them an X.

What Have They Got in Common?

In each row, find the picture that has the most in common with the picture at the left. Circle the box—1, 2, 3, or 4.

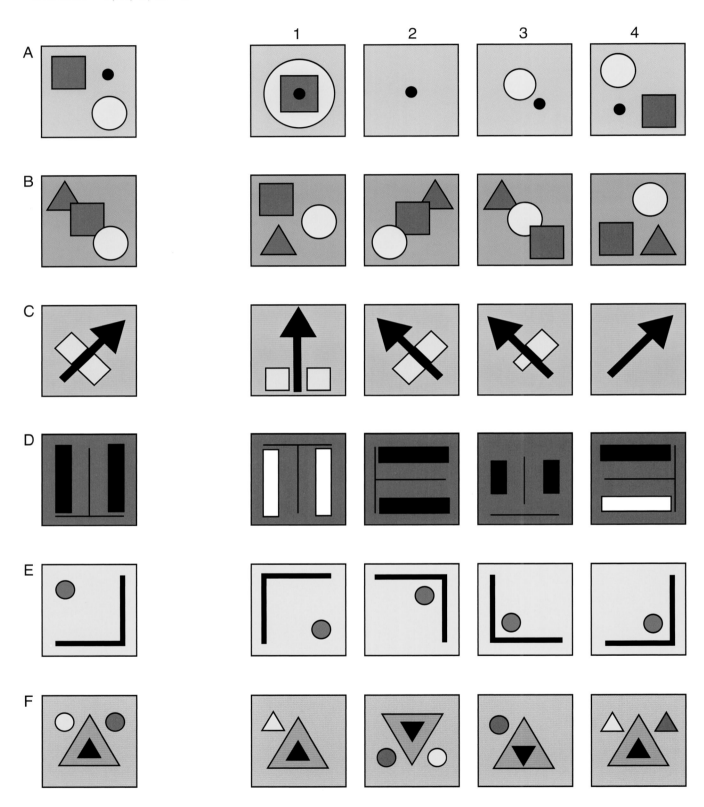

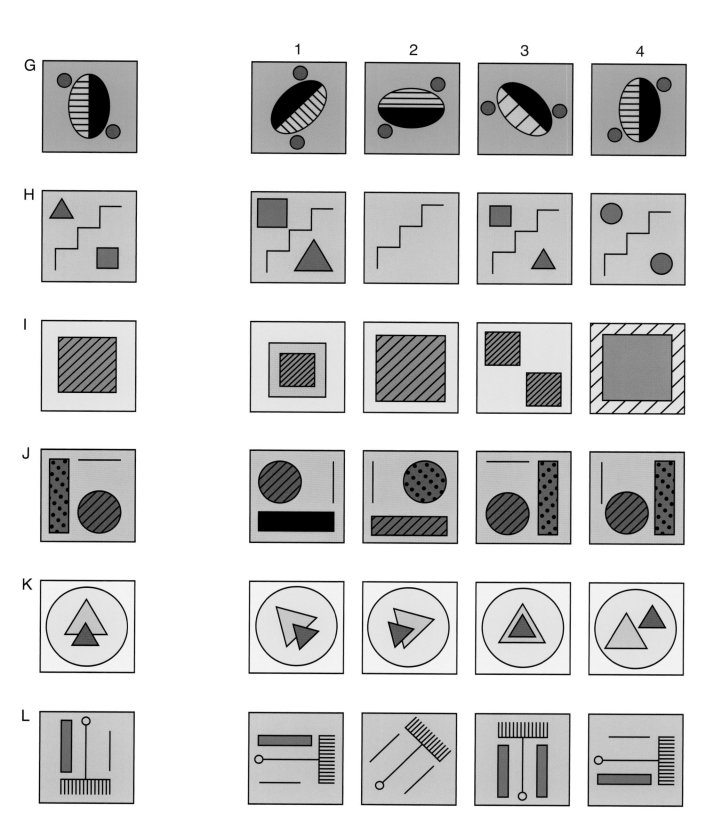

Pencils

Every picture on this page is on page 67, but it has been flip-flopped.
Can you match up the pictures?

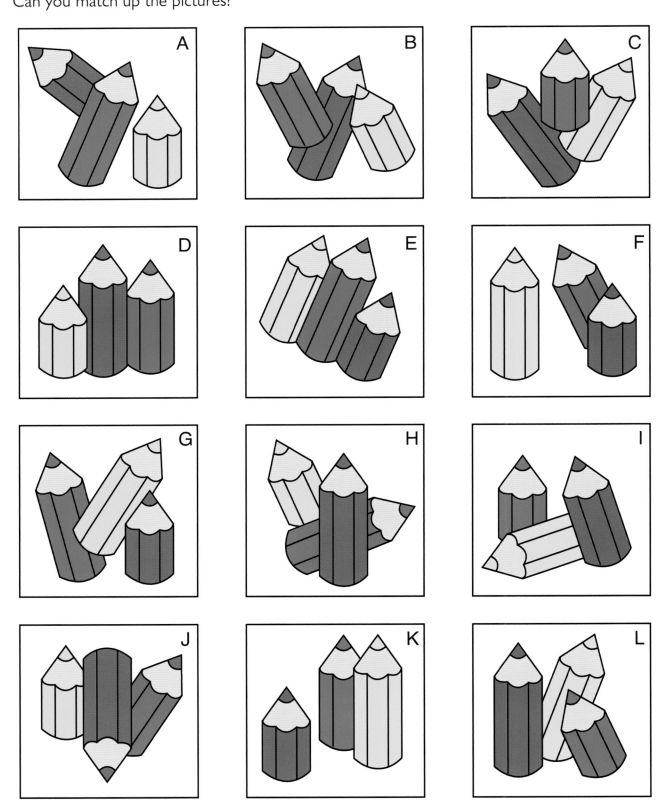

More Mirror Images

Imagine that the long blue line is a mirror. What would appear in the grid below? Choose the right mirror image!

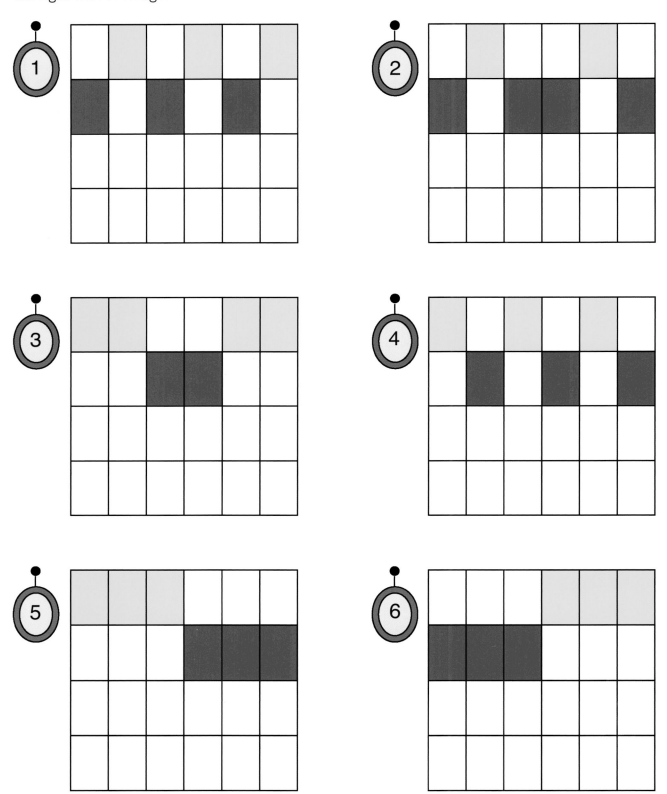

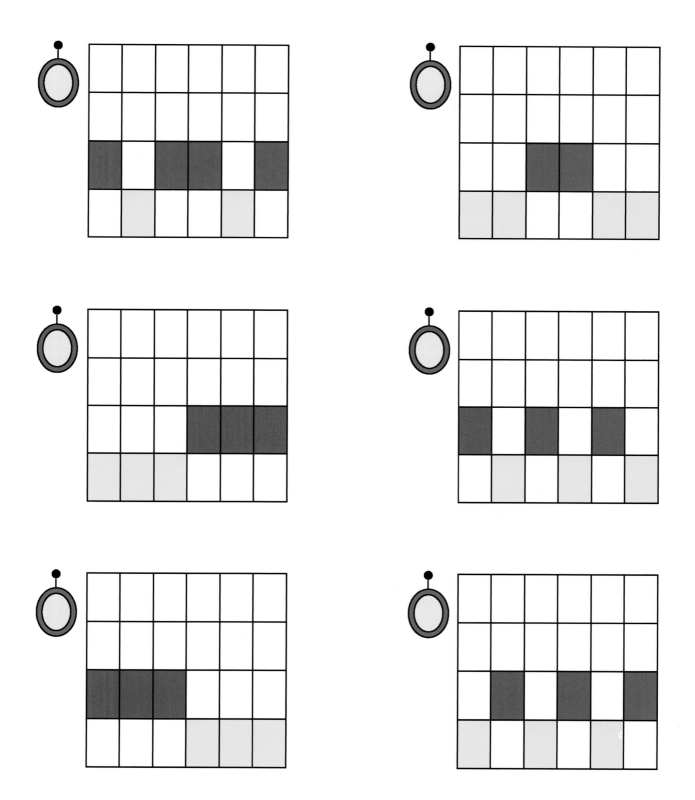

Picture Rows

Which of the two pictures at the right is next?

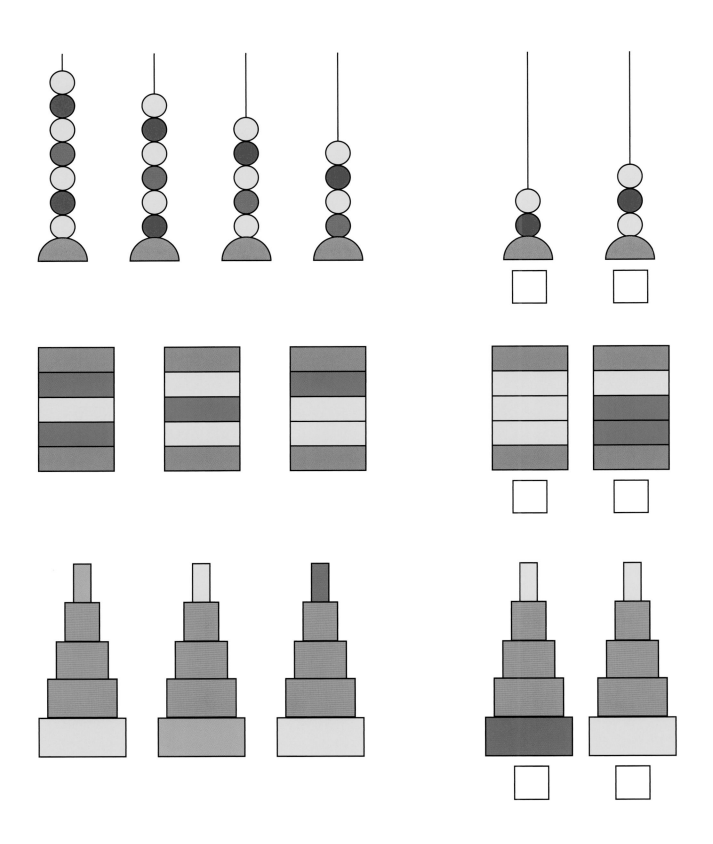

Moving Right Along

How should each line continue? Can you come up with the images that should appear over the dots?

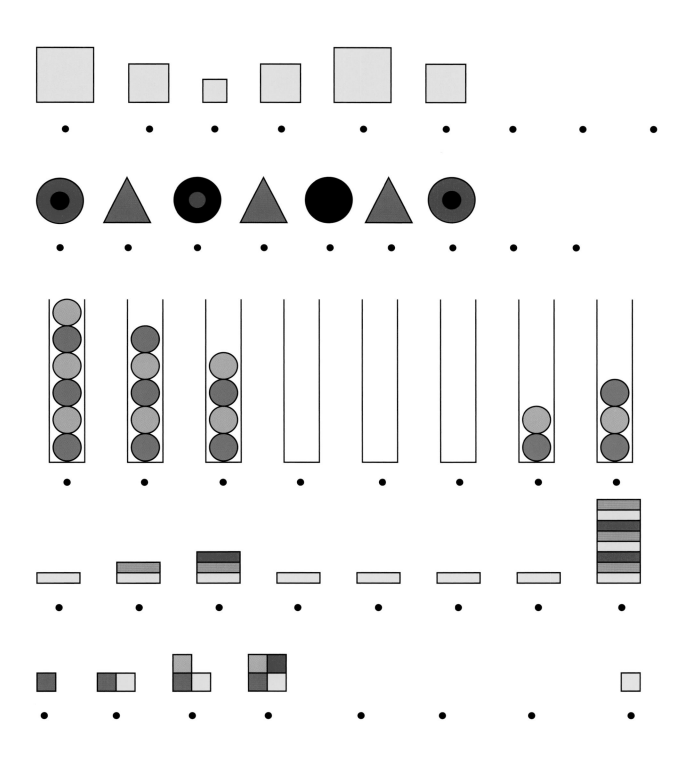

Piece of Cake

Can you find the missing pieces of cake?

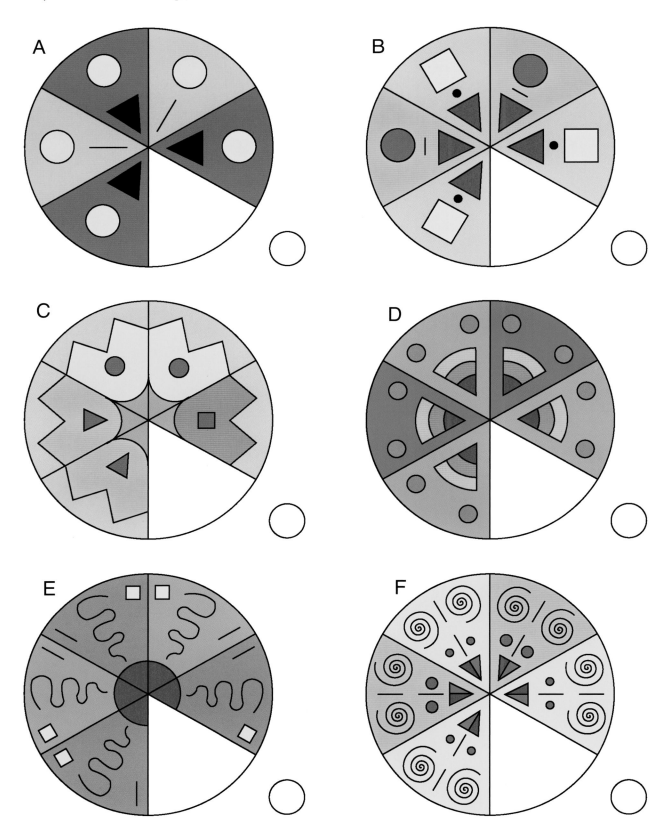

A

B

C

D

E

F

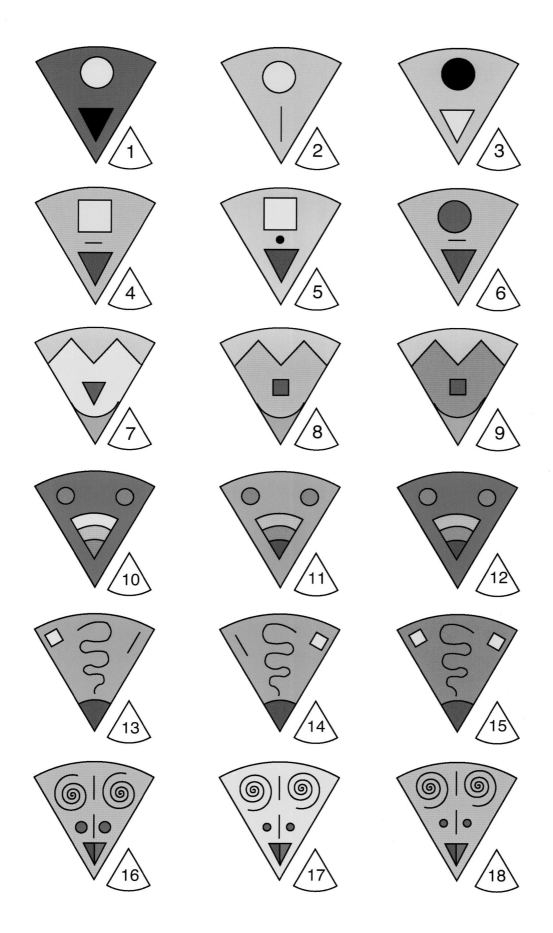

Which Square Fits?

Which square fits in the blank spots? Write the number in the empty space.

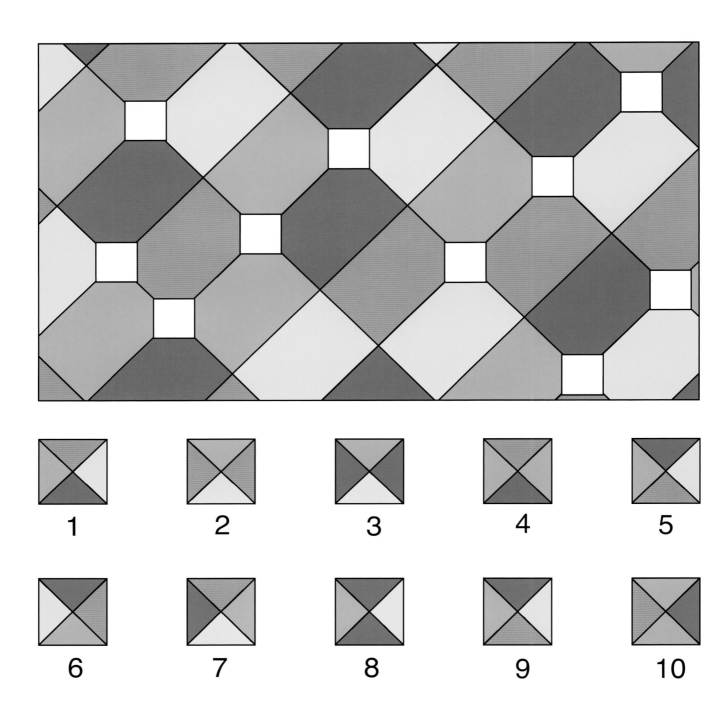

Solutions

Page 5:

9	15	14	12
7	11	2	1
5	13	4	8
6	3	10	16

Page 7:

A		C
F		D
B		E

Page 8-9:

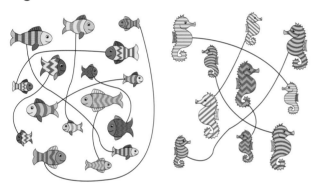

Page 11:

```
G        C
H A      B
  A      E
  D      F
```

Page 13:

```
4  3  5
8  2  9
6  7  1
```

Page 15:

E	H	B
I	A	D
G	C	F

Page 17: A4, B6, C2, D5, E1, F3

Page 19: A3, B5, C7, D6, E9, F1, G8, H2, I4

Page 21: 1A, 2E, 3D, 4C, 5B, 6A

Page 22:

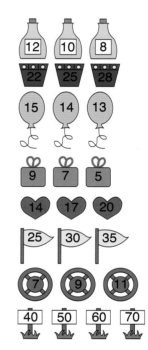

Page 23:

Page 24-25:

Page 26: A D B A B C B A
D C D B

Page 29: Row 1: J, A, F
Row 2: H, G, K
Row 3: I, E, D
Row 4: B, L, C

Page 30:   Row 1: 4, 2, 3, 1
Row 2: 3, 4, 2, 1
Row 3: 3, 1, 2, 4

Page 31:   Row 1: 3, 2, 4, 1
Row 2: 2, 4, 3, 1
Row 3: 3, 4, 2, 1

Page 33:   1st row: Hal, Ellen, Jane
2nd row: Josh, Dan, Liz
3rd row: Adam, Ken, Paul

Page 34:   1B, 2Y, 3B, 4O, 5E, 6T

Page 35:

Page 37:   A1, B5, C2, D6, E4, F3

Page 38:   A5, B9, C12, D2, E1, F11,
G8, H15, I7, J4, K6, L13,
M14, N10, O3.

Page 40:   1b, 2c, 3d, 4a, 5a, 6d, 7c, 8b,
9b, 10a, 11b, 12d, 13b, 14a, 15c

Page 42:   A7, B11, C1, D10, E3, F12,
G5, H6, I9, J8, K2, L4

Page 44:   A1, B15, C8, D16, E5, F11,
G20, H2, I19, J3, K18, L6,
M13, N14, O7, P9, Q4, R17,
S10, T12

Page 47:   1J, 2G, 3F, 4I, 5K, 6E, 7B, 8L,
9D, 10C, 11H, 12A

Page 48:   1J, 2G, 3B, 4F, 5Q

Page 50:   1C, 2E, 3B, 4A, 5F, 6D

Page 52:

Page 53:

Page 55:

Page 56:

C		E		A
B		D		F
H		G		I

Page 57:   1B, 2B, 3C, 4C, 5A, 6A

Page 58:
```
1 4 2 3 1 4
3 1 2 4 2 1
2 4 3 1 2 4
3 1 2 4 3 3
1 3 2 1 4 2
4 2 3 3 4 1
```

Page 61:

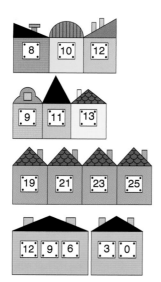

Page 62:

Page 63:

Page 65:

Page 66-67:   A4, B2, C2, D2, E1, F2, G4,
H3, I2, J3, K1, L4

Page 69:
```
B   F   H
C   E   G
J   A   K
I   L   D
```

Page 71:

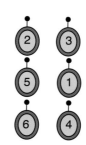

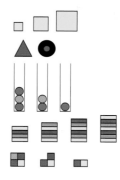

Page 72:

Page 73:

Page 74:   A2, B6, C9, D12, E13, F16

Page 76:

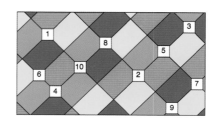

Index

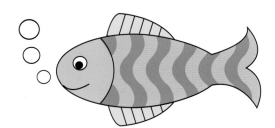